SHREWD AND INNOCENT

A HEART FOR GODLINESS IN ETHICS AND BUSINESS

STEVE COLLIER

MARS HILL PUBLISHING

To my daughters Lindsay, Christen and Brooke:
Thank you for inspiring me.

To my brother Tom Collier:
Many of the ideas presented in this book have come from
our long and wonderful discussions over lunch. Thank you for
being one of my closest friends.

To my father Carroll Collier:
Thank you for showing me how to seek the truth—
no matter the cost.

To my mother Mildred Collier:
Thank you for being the loving foundation for our family.

To my wife Barby:
Thank you for accepting my proposal over 33 years
ago and lovingly being part of God's work in my life
from that day forward. There are no words to
express my gratitude.

A very special thank you to my colleagues who provided much
needed support and feedback during the various stages of this
project (in alphabetical order): Vaughn Akins, Rick Archer,
Vaughn Brock, Dennis Broughton, Taylor Clark, Grant Collier,
Richard Colquitt, Pete Craycroft, Mike Crockett, Thad
Gilliam, William Glasgow, Greg Grooms, Rob Harrell, Britt
Harris, Scot Krieger, Lindsay and Jeremy Martin, Randy and,
Jenna McEachern, Gary Runn, Doug Sherman, Wes Spradley,
Jim Stafford, Scott Sterling, and Scott and Evelyn Tarbell.

TABLE OF CONTENTS

1
Shrewd & Innocent
The Introduction

"Unless someone can find a way to change human nature, we will have more (economic) crisis." Alan Greenspan, former chairman of the U.S. Federal Reserve commenting on the 2009 recession

"The Roots of Violence: Wealth without work, Pleasure without conscience, Knowledge without character, Commerce without morality..." Mahatma Ghandi, Five of his Seven Deadly Sins

"I'm sending you out like sheep among the wolves, so be as shrewd as snakes and as innocent as doves." Jesus' warning to his disciples before their first public assignment (Matthew 10:16)

THE INTRODUCTORY DREAM

It was a very large room with walls covered in carved stone, tall stained glass windows, and a ceiling so high it faded into dark rafters. At the front, on a wide stage, stood two men presiding over hundreds of people moving among aisles and seats. One of the men was informally dressed with a collared shirt, no tie, a sports jacket and scuffed-up shoes. He appeared to be a pastor. The man standing next to him was clothed in a gold trimmed white robe wearing a tall hat that came to a point at the top. It was the Pope!

The people moving around the room were fairly nondescript. They were of all ages, some dressed in suits and ties, others in dresses, and many in shorts and tee-shirts. Some would get up from their seats, go to the stage, mill around for a while, and then a few would leave through the back door while others would come in from the front to take their places.

Most of the people remained quietly seated on white folding chairs, all neatly arranged in arched rows with one large center aisle where the more intense "milling" took place. There had to be around a thousand people with maybe 200 continuously moving, back and forth, from seat to aisle. The Pastor and the Pope stood at the front, smiled, watched, and occasionally gave a few helpful directions.

Then a tall, mustached man with graying hair sitting in the middle of the room stood up to address the crowd. He cleared his throat and spoke loudly to overcome the noise. "Excuse me! Excuse me! I have something to say."

With his polite outburst all the movement slowly ground to a halt. The entire room grew quiet and everyone turned their eyes his way. You could almost count the seconds it took the echo of his voice to fade away into the rafters above.

"With all respect, I have a question." And with this, the Pastor and the Pope turned their attention to him and smiled. They knew this man.

"You know I admire you two men a great deal, and I wouldn't want your jobs for anything. The pressure you guys are under would implode most men, but I feel it's time to speak up.

"You know me, and you know I love the cause we all work for. Most of the people here know me too—that I'm not one to make trouble. But something has been on my mind over the last few years, and it's difficult to bring up."

As he paused, he looked around the room and felt the pleasant and supportive focus of everyone. It's amazing how much easier it is to speak in front of a crowd of familiar faces and genuinely kind hearts.

"Do you remember when we had that special presentation last week? A young man and woman came on stage to announce that they were sensing a call, a deep inner nudge, to go to Africa and serve as missionaries. One was a plumber and the other a schoolteacher. We had a small but moving ceremony and officially sent them off with our prayers and support. We made a big deal out of it—and for good reason.

"Please don't misunderstand what I'm about to say here. I'm as pleased as anyone that these wonderful people want to serve others. We should celebrate anyone who makes a sacrifice like theirs'. And nothing was said to make me feel this way.

"But what does this little ceremony say about the plumbers and schoolteachers who stay behind? I know it says a lot about how important a missionary is, and I'm all behind it, but what does it say about the rest of us?"

He paused again, looking around at the people in the room. "Is God more pleased with them than us? Are we who remain behind, those of us who are not full-time, professional Christians by implication second-class spiritual citizens?

"I know some missionaries who have finished their work and come back home, but I don't recall their being a special ceremony celebrating their return—their return to a new and different call—to join the rest of us in the working world. Should we be disappointed that they returned home with a subtle implication that they failed?"

A low displeasing murmur then arose from those milling around the stage. But the majority who remained seated stayed quiet, still staring at him, but now with strangely hopeful eyes—as if he'd struck a resonant chord and asked a question they secretly wished they had.

The Pope nudged the Pastor, holding back a grin as though saying, "Ha! He must be one of yours."

The Pastor's smile went away and his eyes left the man. He looked slightly downward—not in disgust or anger but pondering the truth in his friend's words, and realizing the fact that he felt strong enough to voice them. They knew each other well. The Pastor knew there was no animosity or offense in his words, and no offense was taken. He was just taking in a loving rebuke, the exposing of a blind spot from someone who loved him. The Pastor had always admired those who made sacrifices similar to his, a call into full-time ministry, and he always praised them publicly. But he never thought that by elevating them as he did he may be devaluing those whose call is different than his own—those who may be just as dedicated.

Then to everyone's surprise the man didn't sit down. He kept speaking.

"I have another concern. Again given with all respect and honor.

"Most of the time our church's teaching deals with the spiritual aspects of our lives—our shortcomings that some call sin, and what we do about it. Seldom are the difficult decisions that stare me in the face each day ever discussed, nor are they even mentioned. The moral and ethical questions about my work, and how I deal with them, seem to be ignored. If I slightly exaggerate my product's positives and diminish their negatives, am I lying? If I'm supposed to love my neighbor as myself, how do I compete with him for the same job? Is it wrong to go into debt? Is it greedy for me to desire a higher salary? Are these issues never discussed because you, my respected and theologically trained leaders, have never really walked in my shoes?

"The church is great at educating in the simple things—love God, obey the Ten Commandments—you know, the don't lie, don't steal stuff. But it seems that's as far as it goes, simple stories, simple answers for simple lives."

Now both the Pastor and the Pope began to look concerned, but they kept listening and their friend spoke up one last time.

"I have one last question for you two, my friends. Well, several actually, but they all boil down to a common concern.

"I understand the importance of pastors, priests and

missionaries. I definitely understand the need for spiritual leaders. We need men and women with hearts dedicated to God with skills in education and counseling, but all this revolves around the spiritual side of life.

"What about the normal, work-a-day, material side of our lives. Is it important? The world where we wake up each morning, eat breakfast, fight traffic, put our noses to the grindstone all day with a couple of short breaks, and then fight the traffic home to focus on the remaining hours of life? If the material life is unimportant, then why do we spend so much of our time on it—fixing pipe, teaching children, programming computers or cleaning the house?

"My life seems so unspiritual, so materialistic compared to yours. But not everyone can quit and join you. If we did, who would be left to grow our food, make our clothes, or work to pay all our salaries?"

FOUNDATIONS

When putting together this first chapter I started with the dream because I wasn't sure how to raise a complaint with the modern church without coming across as a divisive troublemaker. I am neither. As flawed at it is, I still love the church and remain an active leader in it.

I am a full-time businessman with employees, partners, clients and payroll. But I've also been a student of theology nearly all of my live. I love seeking the truth—the bald-faced, unashamed, sometimes ugly yet most times beautiful, no matter where it comes from, the thing that sets you free—truth.

I come from a family of truth seekers—it's a family sport. After Thanksgiving dinner some families put down their knives and forks, run to the television and watch their favorite football game. My family on the other hand scarfs down Thanksgiving dinner in order to remain around the

table and discuss the world and its difficult realities—
politics, spirituality, problems with religion, and problems
with people—and all this without getting into arguments
or raising our voices. It's true. It can actually happen. Not
bad for a group that leans in all philosophical directions—
semi-Buddhists, agnostics, questioning atheists, Mary Baker
Eddy disciples in Christian Science, and evangelical Christ
followers. (I must mention, however, that after exercising
our brains on lofty subjects, our minds eventually grow weary and we leave to watch a game.)

Some call us intellectuals, but they flatter us. In my experience there are only three types of intellectuals. There are
true intellectuals who actually know what they are talking
about. There are pseudo-intellectuals, who put on a good
front, use big words stringing long sentences together and
claim to know what they are talking about—but actually
don't. Then there are hyper-intellectuals, whose hyperactive
minds become full of deep thoughts creating a traffic jamb,
but whose mental engines keep running and seldom arrive
at a destination. Our family falls mostly in the last category.

We can blame my father and mother for all this—both the
yearning for truth and the manner in which we pursue it (in
family peace and intense curiosity).

My father is an artist and has been all his life. He is
also a deeply spiritual man, and he believes in a higher
power—a God who is love. Like most artists he loves new
and alternative ideas. When he was in his thirties and involved in a very conservative church, he spoke up about
some ideas that diverged a little from local church theology, and unfortunately felt the wrath of those less
open-minded. The leaders asked him to leave, and he
eventually booted the whole world of religion. My heart
still aches when I hear him talk about that time in his
life. There was no heresy, no theological bomb thrown
into the congregation, just some interesting ideas worth

examining. Philosophical artists tend to do this, and suffer the consequences.

After World War II and his return home from the army, he was reintroduced to his sister's friend, a beautiful young woman who he soon married. My mother was the first born of four daughters, intelligent, realistic, and bold—similar to many artists' wives. My parents prove opposites do attract—the "big idea" artist and the "show me how it will work before we do it" spouse, the "shake the foundation" artist and the "isn't a foundation kind-of important" spouse. And after more than sixty years of marriage, six children, 14 grandchildren and 10 great grandchildren, wars, economic cycles, death of family members and friends, the artist has been pressed into hard realities while keeping his visionary spark, and the spouse has learned to dream with both feet firmly on the ground. If my father is the creative philosopher, my mother is the loving foundation.

SPORT

With a mother five feet, four inches tall and a father five feet eleven, why I grew to be six feet, three inches and 220 pounds is a mystery to me. I was the mutant child of the family, and for some reason I was also fast.

My mutantness started to become obvious when I was a sophomore in high school. Having played quarterback until that year, I was big enough to be on the varsity team but not experienced enough to play quarterback, so they assigned me to linebacker on defense. One game early in the season, our starting running back left with an injury, and the coach threw me into the game. Several touchdowns and almost 200 rushing yards later, the coach decided I was a running back, and by the end of that year I received my first letter from a college - the perennial contender for the NCAA national football championship, the University of Oklahoma. By the end of high school I had been recruited by most every major university in the country. Who knew this would come to a mutant son of an artist?

My claim to fame came when the University of Texas football coach Darrell Royal flew into Dallas, drove through my small town of Forney (a blink of an eye 15 miles east on I-20), to sign me to a scholarship while he was on his way to sign another running back, Earl Campbell.

Earl was an uncomplicated, decent man who God touched and made the mutant of all mutant running backs. Without lifting weights he was all muscle and could run sideways faster than I could run forward. He went on to win the Heisman Trophy and join the NFL Hall of Fame. Earl and I met at the Texas High School Football All-Star Game where we were in the same backfield and on a team with ten or more other UT signees. Later Earl and I met again to compete for the same running back position our freshman year. Let's just say Earl won, and I ended up playing defense—with the honor of starting as a free safety as a sophomore.

With a few minor exceptions, I had the privilege of playing under some of the best coaches and along side some of the best players in college football. We ended my senior year when we met Joe Montana of Notre Dame in the national championship game. Unfortunately, I had injured my knee at the beginning of the season and watched the game from the press box. The Longhorns lost.

Afterward I said goodbye to football and continued on the alternative path I had been pursuing while at college—architecture. Football gave me just a small taste of fame. I had my fifteen minutes and I found it not as wonderful or easy as you would think.

TO WORK

There is a period of withdrawal when leaving the limelight of University of Texas sports, a cramp in your self-esteem, especially when you've played for a team that's on national television so often and in a stadium that holds more people than most cities in Texas. However, I'm convinced I would be either dead or paralyzed had I played professional football—not that anyone was clamoring extremely hard for me to play.

Coming from an artistic family and graduating high in my class secured me a job with a couple of professors from the architecture school. It was an honor to be chosen, but in reality it was a form of indentured servitude. With a professional degree from a prestigious university, you think I would be paid more than a ditch digger, but that wasn't the case. Three years later, I found myself owner of my own small architectural firm and riding a wave of economic prosperity—at least until a banking crisis shut down the income stream.

The timing of the economic downturn was terrible. It coincided with my purchase of a new house, investment in other real estate, the arrival of my second daughter, the moral failure of a pastor whose mentorship I valued, and the closing of a church in which my wife and I served for years.

Looking back, it appears these years and experiences were preparing me for writing a book such as this. Since then I've had the opportunity to open and close businesses, buy and sell businesses, bring on partners and leave partnerships, hire and (regretfully) fire employees. And on a parallel path to my so-called secular career was the sacred world of ministry. Following my family's passion for the truth, my wife and I followed our hearts to be involved. From running a high school youth program in our spare time, to babysitting, teaching, building campaigns and leadership boards, we have been deeply involved in the world of volunteer ministry.

SHREWD AND INNOCENT

A few years ago, I was reading in the book of Matthew and came upon a verse I had read over many times before, but had never really noticed. Jesus was sending out his disciples for the first time, and he was giving them some advice and a warning.

"I'm sending you out like sheep among the wolves, so be as shrewd as snakes and as innocent as doves." (Matthew 10:16)

Jesus of Nazareth, son of Mary and Joseph who strolled the earth just after the time of Plato and Aristotle, had chosen twelve young men ranging in age from their twenties to early thirties. Some were educated and others simply fishermen. Some were wealthy, others poor, but all were rookies when it came to the work Jesus had in store for them.

What caught my eye was he told them to "be shrewd as snakes?" Where in the world did this come from? It was a mystery to me how something so sinister sounding would come from the mouth of a man who preached love and forgiveness. Where's the love your enemy stuff? Being shrewd was never a trait I admired, much less wanted to emulate, and now Jesus was recommending it to his top twelve. In fact, the mystery got even more fascinating as I studied further. His statement is a direct reference to the Garden of Eden, Adam and Eve, and the snake that was the shrewdest creature God placed there.

Did Jesus actually want these guys to be crafty and cunning like the one who tempted Adam and Eve in the garden? It certainly appeared so. Jesus was definitely no stranger to scripture and knew exactly what he was saying when he told them to be shrewd.

But the rest of the statement is just as confusing. Not only does Jesus tell his young men to be shrewd, they were to be innocent as well. It is a "both/and" statement, not an "either/or." Not shrewd or innocent, but shrewd and innocent (not a naïve sort of innocent, but blameless, as in innocent of a crime).

Now here was a subject a businessperson could sink their teeth into. This was no simple Sunday school lesson. It involved wisdom and balance and making judgment calls. It involved creativity—things I deal with every day.

My world revolves around supply and demand, risk and reward, sales quotas and serving clients. I have to decide how much I should charge for my services. Do I buy insurance to cover the risks of my business or family? Should I lease or buy the copier? What is a reasonable and Godly wage to pay my employees—or myself?

In finding this verse I began to discover a deeper set of realities about the world of business where the truth often gets distorted. Certainly there are a lot of easy black and white truths out there, but the older I get, the more gray I see—with decisions more suited for King Solomon or Einstein than to a simple architect and author like me.

There are wolves out there looking to eat you alive, take your money, your soul, and then go on to the next sheep. So you should be shrewd and innocent—wise, crafty, yet blameless. This should be the credo for all who enter the business world.

But there's a problem. You can't always tell who the wolves are. Sometimes the wolves wear sheep camouflage. Sometimes they travel in packs and are so numerous you can't escape. And, unfortunately, sometimes you find your friend, pastor, or priest is the wolf.

No wonder we need to be as wise and crafty as the most evil of wolves—our very lives are at stake. But in the middle of the messy life of business sales, negotiations, manufacturing, and consulting, we are supposed to be innocent of the very stuff we are told to be aware of. Now that's a challenge worthy of someone in the business world who seeks the truth and wants to do what's right.

MY MISSION

I believe those who have entered the world of business have a special mission—a calling as significant and spiritual as the priesthood or pastorship.

And I'm not alone. Martin Luther backs me up. Luther said the Godly clothier makes clothes "because God has bidden me do so, so that I can earn a living, so that I can help and serve my neighbor."

John Calvin said that when God is his guide, "The magistrate will execute his office with greater pleasure, and the father of a family will confine himself to his duty with more satisfaction."

And there is a sense of freedom when you realize the significance of this special calling—when you match who you are to what you are called to do. Os Guinness said in his book *The Call*, "God does call us to 'be ourselves' and 'do what we are.' But we are only truly 'ourselves' and can only 'do what we are' when we follow God's call. Giftedness that is "ours for others" is therefore not selfishness but service that is perfect freedom."

Do you want to know what freedom feels like—real freedom? It's not having the opportunity to do whatever you want. To some that's freedom, but they miss the real idea. Real freedom is knowing what you ought to do and having the ability to do it. Freedom isn't having the opportunity to drive your car in any direction on a crowded highway—you may never reach your destination. Freedom is the pleasant assurance that you will be able to reach your destination by knowing the direction to travel.

Freedom is not remaining in the insecurity of unanswered questions, including the big existential questions (questions of existence): Why are we here? Where are we going? Freedom is knowing what you're supposed to be doing. It is to know what you were called to do; your mission—the priesthood, the pastorship, an administrative assistant, or a doctor.

I know this definition of freedom may sound a little backward—having someone tell you to do one thing, means you no longer can do the other thing. This seems to restrict freedom. A limitation on life choices doesn't appear to be freedom, but not knowing what to do in this life, beginning one job just to find it is unsatisfying and moving into another, being tossed around by indecision, is no freedom at all. It's unfulfilling aimlessness.

Abraham Lincoln said, "Freedom is not the right to do what we want, but what we ought."

"I will walk about in freedom, for I have sought out you (God)." (Psalms 119:45)

"It is for freedom that Christ has set us free. Stand firm, then, and do not let yourselves be burdened again by a yoke of slavery." (Galatians 5:1)

"Live as free men, but do not use your freedom as a cover-up for evil; live as servants of God." (1 Peter 2:16)

Have you ever been faced with too many choices and paralyzed in your decision of what is best? Do I obey my boss or my conscience? What company should I work for? Should I move to another city for a better job opportunity? Do you feel free?

Ask any recent university graduate entering the work force with every option in the world at his disposal. Does he feel freedom at the myriads of choices before him, or does he feel paralyzed with so many choices and no direction for his life?

Knowing your calling gives your life direction and reveals priorities. When you know where your God-given talent, experience, and heart lead you (whether in the world of construction, teaching or ministry), your choices are easier. Knowing your calling sets you free to enjoy the work in front of you. This is just a glimpse into what scripture calls living by faith.

TWO WORLDS

It appears we are caught in two worlds—the material and the spiritual. In the material world we have ourselves, our fellow humans, our planet, and the tons of work required to maintain them all. We work for money to buy food, housing, computers, and energy. To some this work is satisfying, but only until they ponder the spiritual world and whether this brief life is all there is. In the spiritual world we have our faith, our church and the tons of disciplines require to maintain them—prayer, bible study, and worship. To some this is satisfying, but only until they ponder their hunger and need to make money to meet their real material needs.

I believe these two worlds are closer than you may think. In fact, I think they are linked and inseparable. Doing good work has more spiritual connections than we can fathom, and I hope to prove this to you as you continue reading, because there is no greater satisfaction than knowing your work has spiritual and eternal value.

HUMAN NATURE

While I'm on this earth I want to do the best I can with what I've been given, with the most benefit for the most people. But there are those wolves in my way—so I want to know the ways and wiles of the wolves in this world, but at the same time I don't want to use that knowledge to prey on others. I want to know the dark side, but I don't want to join it. I want to be shrewd and innocent.

There is a disease in the business world and we all know it, but the disease is not money, wealth, fame or any other thing in this world. These are just symptoms of the disease. Alan Greenspan hit the nail on the head. The disease lives within us, our human nature, and unless we cure the disease, fighting the symptoms will be a futile and fruitless effort.

There is good news. There is a cure for human nature, and I pray this book will be a guide in your quest for the cure.

BEFORE THE NEXT CHAPTER—A NOTE TO MY READERS

In my lifetime, I've run across two different types of people—both good but definitely different people. On one side you have the down-to-earth, practical, logical folks who like to get to work—no deep discussions for them. They say, "Just tell me what to do and I'll do it. We've found that after doing something for a while, we then begin to understand why we're doing it. So don't confuse us with all that philosophical stuff." These are the needed and beloved left-brained, linear thinkers—many are engineers, construction workers, and accountants.

A good friend of mine was a runner—sweating through miles every day throughout college. He loved it. To me, however, running was a punishment created by coaches. "That's two laps for you, Collier!" Several years after my friend graduated and as I watched him continue his running, I asked him why he kept doing it. He looked at me as if I had asked why he kept breathing.

Then a few weeks later he walked up to me and confessed, "You know Steve, I was on my fourth mile the other day and I remembered your question. And I couldn't think of a good reason for running miles and miles every day. So I just stopped there in my tracks. I didn't have a good answer."

I apologized, but he thanked me anyway. He realized he wanted to spend that time doing other, more important things—spending time with his family and study to advance his career. He didn't stop running all together, he just put it in the right relationship to other priorities.

On the other side you have the right-brained, nonlinear thinkers—many who are artists, theoretical scientists, and economists. They are the ones who, in the middle of a conversation, suddenly lose their train of thought because they remembered where they left their cell phone two days ago. But if you ask them why they do what they do, they will tell you quickly, and thoroughly.

If you find yourself in the linear thinker camp, you may want to start with Part Two of this book and get directly into the details. Then afterward, if your curiosity overcomes you, you may want to come back to Part One—so when you begin wondering why you are doing all these things, you won't stop in your tracks.

But for the nonlinear thinkers, just continue. As you will find, like many architects, my brain leans toward the philosophical. But the realities of life have taught me some hard lessons. We can talk all day about the philosophy of roof design, but unless someone studies the details and installs it correctly, the roof leaks.

Part One

SIMPLE PHILOSOPHY

Looking at the Forest from 30,000 feet

2
Why Are We Here?
The Naturals

"Why are we here? Funny how just because we're capable of asking the question, we assume there's an answer. We are a self aware chemical reaction. We replicate, therefore we are." Matthew Keith Groves, his "Little Rave about A Forward Thinking Philosophy" expresses the sentiment of many modern people

"The meaning of life? It's nothing very special...Uh, try to be nice to people, avoid eating fat, read a good book every now and then, get some walking in, and try to live together in peace and harmony with people of all creeds and nations." Michael Palin of Monty Python on his film "The Meaning of Life"

"If a man will begin with certainties, he shall end in doubts, but if he will be content to begin with doubts, he shall end in certainties." Sir Francis Bacon, English author and philosopher from his work on "The Advancement of Learning"

THE QUESTION

Why?

That's my favorite question.

Of all the questions you can ask—who, what, when, where, why, how and how much—why has driven my curiosity as long as I can remember. If you're like me, you're a why person.

My wife on the other hand is a who person. She's amazing. She remembers who everyone is—knows everyone's name.

She remembers the names of distant relatives (my distant relatives), even those I can't remember myself. She thrives on helping others, learning about others, counseling others, myriads of others. I, on the other hand, do know a few people, but I still lean on my wife when it comes to...that person coming toward me with a knowing smile. "Psssst...Steve... that's your aunt Edith." "Thank you lovely wife."

You also have the what, when and where people—the historians of the world. They love what happened, where it happened, and when it happened. Don't get them started on the Civil War unless you have several hours.

Then there are the how and how much people—the scientists, engineers, economists and accountants.

Scientists and engineers spend their lives figuring out how things work and defining the nature of the universe. Their work is fascinating and I must admit I have how tendencies when I hear these guys discuss the make up of DNA or the future of technology.

Economists and accountants, on the other hand, are the most confusing of all question askers. Have you ever met an economist? Who can understand these guys? I've taken my share of economics courses, played with supply and demand as well as Keynesian and classical economic theories, but who really cares?

My wife can tell you who these economists are. The scientist can tell you how an economist's brain works. The historian can tell you what economist came up with a theory, when it was published and where it influenced the financial world.

But I look at all this and ask...why?

WHAT WHY TELLS YOU

Let me explain a little further why answering the question why is so important.

Say I was in my office and called out to you in the room

next door, "Hey, you (whatever your name is). Would you get me a glass of water?"

Now if you were a considerate person, as you probably are, you would get up from your chair, walk to the kitchen, find a glass, pour some water in it, then walk to my room, and hand it to me.

As you were getting the water, you had answers to most of your internal who, what, when, and where questions.

Who is the needy person? That author in the other room.

What does he want? He specifically asked for water.

When does he want it? It appears he wants it right now.

Where is the water? The last time you got a glass it was in the kitchen.

How and how much? He said he wanted one glass worth and you've poured water before, so you know how to do it.

Why?

Well, you have to make an assumption here. Does he need to water his favorite plant? Does he want to put the glass in the window and watch the pretty prismatic colors light the wall? Is he thirsty? The last one is the most likely reason, so you go to your task accordingly.

But what if I told you I needed the glass of water because, "MY HAIR IS ON FIRE!"

My guess is your entire attitude about the water retrieving would change drastically. These five little words would give a whole new meaning to your task.

By knowing why you would make entirely different decisions. You would walk faster, or even run to the kitchen, grab the first glass you see instead of searching for a clean one in the cabinet, dump the water into the glass, and splash every object in the way as you ran back to deliver the fire quenching liquid.

With this little, but extremely important, piece of why information, you found new meaning—a guiding principle. This guiding principle directs your actions to what you ought to do (run) and what you ought not do (walk slowly).

That's what why does. It gives you the ought in your tasks.

Not so with the other questions. They just provide facts. Who wanted what, when and where did he want it? These are just fact questions. They are important questions for sure. Facts are extremely important. (If you didn't know what to do, what would you do? You'd do nothing).

But these fact questions don't give you the all important reason—why. If you ask a scientist, "Why is the sky blue?" He will describe the molecular make up of the air and the spectral make up of the light passing through it causing our eyes to observe the color we call blue. But that is the answer to a how question—not the why question that gives the reason for it. "Why is the sky blue?" Only the thing that created it can answer that question.

Facts just tell you what exists, what is, not what ought to be.

Bottom line? Why guides you. It reveals priorities. It explains motivations. Unless you know why you go to work everyday, to church, or attend school, these tasks will have no real meaning. Without meaning, working everyday will become monotonous and unfulfilling. Without meaning, going to church is an empty ritual, and going to school is a wasted mental exercise.

THE BIG WHY QUESTION

But now to the question at hand: Why are we here?

There is no bigger why question.

If we can answer this why question, we can understand what is really important. We can find the guiding principles for life, and understand what our priorities ought to be. It can give our life meaning.

"But wait," you may be asking. "Isn't this a little too simplistic?" Some of you may think I'm pulling the intellectual wool over your eyes; attempting some logical slight of hand.

But I'm not. It's relatively easy, really—the meaning of life thing. But since I know there are skeptics out there let's take this why question in two directions. There are many schools of thought but let's just deal with the two prominent ones— two families I'll call the Naturals and the Spirituals.

There are many in the Naturals family who would say, "Mr. Collier, you can't ask this big WHY question. By doing so you are quietly implying that there is someone or something out there to answer it. You are implying that there is a person, a God, someone with a mind, a who, who can answer. We Naturals only believe in what we can see, touch or probe scientifically. We believe in a closed universe—a closed system of matter and energy, with no influence from anyone or anything outside." They agree with Carl Sagan when he said, "For me, it is far better to grasp the universe as it really is than to persist in delusion, however satisfying and reassuring."

Yes, you caught me. By suggesting that there is an answer to the why question, I'm implying there is something out there who can answer—a someone with a motive. A rock or a star or any other lifeless object can't have a motive. A something (as opposed to a someone) can't intend to do anything. Only a person or a being with some mental capacity can give a reason, have a motive, or provide a guiding principle for any why question. By asking, "Why are we here?" I am exposing a very big division in thought. On one side the Naturals will say, "The big WHY question makes no sense, because there is no one there to answer it."

For everyone in the Naturals family, let me say that I respect your point of view. I enjoy talking to people who have a thoughtful view of the world which may differ from my own. It's refreshing to hear new and different ideas that either confirm or contradict mine. Such ideas always strengthen my ideas for the better—either by changing, modifying or confirming them. But it's not refreshing talking to people with ideas that contradict themselves, or those who can't or don't live consistently with their point of view. These guys will say whatever they can to justify their choices, and this goes for both the Naturals and the Spirituals. As a philosopher once said, "A man's morality dictates his philosophy." In other words, we all like to justify our actions.

MORAL INTELLIGENCE – A CASE FOR THE NATURALS

Can we have a guiding principle, an answer to the why question that gives the ought to our lives, without something or someone there to tell us?

Many anthropologists say, "Of course you can. Just observe the way people live across vast cultural boundaries."

In their article entitled A Short List of Universal Moral Principals, professors Kinnier, Kernes, and Dautheribes describe this common or universal ought to life—morality. "Genuine differences in behavior in different cultures may distract us from what we have in common with all people—a universal moral compass. Consider a study that compared children in India with American children. The differences in values were predictable: Indian children displayed more deference to elders and acceptance of tradition, while American children valued personal autonomy and freedom. But their moral codes were virtually identical. Both groups of children believed that it was wrong to lie, cheat, steal, and both thought that it was important to treat the sick or unfortunate with kindness."

Their research shows a majority of the world's societies have very similar attitudes when it comes to what is right and wrong. By statistical research they found that most societies do not accept lying, cheating, stealing personal property, or murder. By definition these are morally wrong.

I've observed this myself. I know people who live good, moral lives who don't believe in a supreme being, a mystical moral force, or anything else beyond this physical universe. Yet they give to charities and are kind to their neighbors.

And strangely enough these universal moral codes also hold true for what most of us would call immoral people—organized crime. Even those who are not known for their high moral standards still hold to the same sense of right and wrong. Even though they lie, steal, and murder others, they would take great offense if someone lied to or stole from them, or murdered one of their loved ones. They are not good people, but they still expect moral behavior within their own group—a strange perverted "honor among thieves." So the observation that humankind has an inner guiding principle or morality has validity.

But how can these social scientists conclude that we all know right from wrong? How did they come to their conclusions?

They took a scientific poll. They simply polled different cultures around the world with a majority responding that steeling, lying, and murdering were "wrong." That's what scientists do. They ask how questions, not why questions.

But can we actually determine what is right and wrong from a poll? Don't polls just confirm what is popular at any a certain time? Thousands of years ago, sacrificing children was a popular practice in some societies, as well as prostitution. In mid 19th century China the use of opium led to half its population becoming addicted to the popular drug. Hitler was put into office by a poll called the vote.

Determining right and wrong from a poll has some real problems. "OK...Everyone in favor of stealing from the rich, or stealing from the poor, or stealing from the government, raise your hand." We all know there's something very wrong with this. "Everyone in favor of sending all Naturals to prison, raise your hand." Popularity just tells us what or who is popular at the moment. A poll just states what is, and you can't get ought from is.

What if a majority of society's citizens lived very different lives. Let's assume lying, stealing, and murder were common and accepted behaviors. If this were so and the social scientists used their same methodology, they would have to conclude that lying, steeling and murder were good and acceptable.

The fact is that observation can only generate statistics—facts and what is. They can't conclude what is right or wrong. Their conclusions are purely a hopeful, speculative, leap of faith that humankind has a universal guiding principle—a common sense of ought.

When you believe, as the Naturals do, that the universe is a closed system with no influence from any metaphysical or spiritual dimension, all you can do is observe the facts, and make assumptions. You can never get to what really ought to be.

The Naturals have read Charles Darwin (a brilliant observer and thinker but not necessarily a Natural) and concluded that survival is what is right and good. What makes us survive is right and what keeps us from surviving is wrong—survival of the fittest and natural selection. What we ought to do is what allows us to survive. This is a consistent conclusion any Natural can come to, although they may not like some of its potentially brutal ramifications.

When you're a Natural, all there is, is what you perceive with your senses. There's nothing outside. "I am born. I eat, sleep, marry, have children, enjoy some moments, and survive for a few decades. When I die, I'm no longer here, so I no longer exist." There is no one "out there" telling me right from wrong. We are basically advanced creatures, seeking to survive and find a few moments of pleasure. And if all you have are facts in a closed universe with no one outside telling you what you ought or ought not do, all you can do is decide for yourself what you ought to do—what is right and wrong.

MY PERSONAL CRISIS

Remember when you used to ask your parents (or tortured your parents with) the question why?

"Dad, why is the grass green?"

If your father wanted to answer honestly and not simply pacify you, he'd say, "Well, little person, the sunlight hits the grass, and the color green bounces back."

"Why does green bounce back?" you would then ask.

"Well, sunlight has all the colors of the rainbow and the grass is made in such a way that it absorbs all the colors except green," he would say.

"Why?"

"Well, the molecular make up of the grass and the wavelength or speed of the photons..." You can take the conversation from there.

Eventually, either because you pushed him past his knowledge of the subject or because you pushed him past his threshold of patience, the inevitable concluding remark would come—"Just because I told you so" or "You're going to have to trust me on this one." Your father either couldn't go past the conundrum of wave and particle theory, or he knew you were too young to understand the real answer anyway. So he just suggested you trust him that there was an answer.

This type of answer satisfied me through high school and my freshman year of college. But when I grew to be a sophomore and was exposed to ideas beyond my father's counsel, the crisis began. I realized I was answering my why question with a how answer. The molecular makeup of grass only tells how it is green—not why. And my questions were moving from grass and sky to my very reasons for existence. Why am I here? Where did we all come from? If it all came from the Big Bang then where did the stuff of the Big Bang come from? Has everything always been here—an infinity before us? No longer did the "trust me" answers satisfy anymore.

Why am I here? Why is evil in the world? Why do I desire to do what is wrong, and what can I do about? These questions plagued me.

For months I didn't get any answers, and later the answers I did receive, "God made the universe in six 24 hour days" didn't match my science classes. "Evil came from Satan, or our own selfish desires," or "there is no such thing as evil. There are only choices without morality." My favorite answer was, "You must be 'in sin' to have doubts like that." Looking back, I see this as one of the pivotal moments in my life. Do I blindly accept the apparent naïve faith of my past or do I dump it all and start my own quest for the truth? This was a dark time, but looking back, I wish everyone would go through such a time of faith testing.

I then found a book by an American philosopher Francis Schaeffer, who lived and taught in Switzerland, The book was entitled *He is There and He is Not Silent*. It took a month of reading with a dictionary by my side (I'd never used words like epistemological, a-priori, or anthropomorphic), but the ideas and answers started coming. Not all the answers, but the foundational ones which spoke reasonably to a view of the world with something or someone outside the system, beyond the matter and energy we perceive with our senses.

Since then I've read philosophers, scientists, theologians, and artists with world views in stark contrast to the Naturals—legitimate, thoughtful and consistent world views. Views that account for the ought that resonates within me, the communal sense of right and wrong regarding lying, theft, murder, and more.

3
Why Are We Here?
The Spirituals

"Concern for man and his fate must always form the chief interest of all technical endeavors. Never forget this in the midst of your diagrams and equations." Albert Einstein in his address to the California Institute of Technology entitled Science and Happiness

"Which is it. Is man one of God's blunders, or is God one of man's blunders?" Friedrich Nietzsche from his book, "Twilight of the Idols or How to Philosophize with a Hammer" (1889)

"To one who has faith, no explanation is necessary. To one without faith, no explanation is possible." St. Thomas Aquinas, 13th century Italian priest, Dominican philosopher and theologian

THE MORAL BEING – A CASE FOR THE SPIRITUALS

Have you ever wondered where male and female came from? If we all started from a single cell reproductive organisms (a pretty efficient system by the way), what happened to make us move to a new, less efficient system of having to rely on another person to reproduce?

What bolt of lightning hit a DNA strand millions of years ago and caused it to split into two exactly perfect halves (the way DNA actually splits in human reproduction). At another time, another mutation caused a cell to split exactly into a perfect, but exactly opposite, half of the same DNA sequence (an exact sequence—hundreds of pieces long with each piece lining up exactly with the other strand of DNA). Then these two semi-DNA strands from different cells don't die off, but find each other and have the audacity to combine their perfect halves to form the possibility of another complete cell with all the building blocks to create another incredibly complex life form. Now that is magical. What are the odds?

Why doesn't the fossil record reveal any concise missing links from ape to man (do your research), or from any species to a higher developed species—anywhere? Scientists say it takes thousands of mutations to move from one species to another—from fish to amphibian, from ape to man. If this were true, wouldn't there be mounds of fossil evidence showing minor sequences of the evolutionary process?

Darwin himself spoke in "The Origins of Species" about these gaps in the fossil records, "Geology assuredly does not reveal any such finely graduated organic chain; and this, perhaps, is the most obvious and serious objection which can be urged against the theory [of evolution]." Even Darwin knew his scientific limits.

These what, where and how questions are fascinating, numerous, and actually beyond the scope of this book. But the facts are, the more we understand the make up of the vast universe and the more we observe details of microbiology, the more facts point to a something or someone that caused it. The more I study and the more I observe, the more I'm convinced that there is something or someone who stepped into the system, into the universe. And the deciding factor is not purely scientific. It is within the world of observation, logic and reason for sure, but it is something more, and it resonates within me.

There are many ways to argue for the existence of some-thing or someone that caused it all, and there are hundreds of books arguing both sides, but there is one thing that tips the scales. It's something you know is true deep within your gut. You know it's true the same way the closed universe Naturals know the things they believe are true. They believe something came from nothing, and that there is no real cause or meaning in this random universe. But where they see chaos theory, I see unity. Where they see spontaneous generation, I see someone with an artist's eye for creativity. Most assuredly the evidence we observe must match the reason and logic in our minds, but eventually it's our beliefs, our hearts, that make the final decision. As the 17th century French scientist and mathematician Blasé Pascal wrote, "The heart has its reasons which reason cannot know."

HE IS THERE

I come from the other family of thought. Let's call them the Spirituals. Just as the Naturals deduce and believe there is nothing beyond our universe, the Spirituals deduce and believe there is something beyond our universe.

Within the Spirituals view of the world, there is a who, who can answer the big question. And since the question is now answerable, we can ask, search, and even find guiding principles—the ought for living our lives.

The case for a creator or a God is a strong one, and the more science expands its knowledge about the vastness of the universe and complexity of life, the evidence mounts. Something can't come from nothing. Something had to be there in the first place. Something or someone has acted and influenced our well-crafted and mechanical universe. In fact, it is so simple and obvious one could easily over look it. If you were walking along a beach, looked down and found a watch still ticking, would you ask yourself, "I wonder how the water and sand managed to form this watch over millions of years? And, it's still ticking!" Or, would you consider that an artist and craftsman used his skills to manipulate metal to form and then wind the spring for it to run?"

HE IS NOT SILENT

The Spirituals case for a creator is a strong one, and it's one thing to conclude a creative being exists. It is one thing to say someone "is there." But it is quite another to say he is "not silent," or that he has been involved in his creation or revealed himself to us using the scriptures as his instrument. How can you prove that?

Well, proof comes by different methods. In order for something to be proven scientifically, it has to be shown true over and over again through experimentation and observation of the facts. You prove water turns red when you add red die to it because you can do it over and over again with the same result. Einstein had his special theory of relativity proven by other scientists photographing the apparent movement of stars when passing by the mass of our sun. Scientific problems need scientific proof.

But how do you prove that Albert Einstein existed? You never met him personally or shook his hand. How do you prove George Washington, Jesus, Plato existed—or your great-grandparents for that matter? You can't come up with an experiment and observe it over and over again; the scientific method fails here.

Instead you depend on other types of evidence—reasonable, reliable and believable evidence. You make a decision based on the evidence you trust and the evidence you throw out. You should trust, but verify the truth. That's the way you prove something that can't be reproduced scientifically—like evaluating evidence in a court of law. You read, test, and trust the words written by Moses and the Jewish historians. You trust the words of Matthew, Mark, Luke, John, Paul, and Peter, who walked and talked with Jesus. You trust the historians, anthropologists, and social scientists who dive into these texts and confirm their authenticity. You examine the evidence behind those men who foretold the exile of Israel, the rebuilding of the Temple, and the coming of the Messiah. And if you are a student or disciple of Jesus of Nazareth, you read, test and trust his words when he refers to scripture as the very words of God—that there is a God and he is not silent.

This creative being is obviously there when we look at the vast complexity and beauty of the universe. I believe it's obvious to an honest and humble person who looks with an open mind and open heart. And this creative being is not silent. He has spoken through special men he loves and chose to be his mouthpieces—Moses, David, the prophets and the Apostles in sixty-six books compiled by wise men under his guidance. And within those writings, we find the answer to our big question.

WHY ARE WE HERE?

The answer to the big WHY question comes in two parts. Not only does it involve our existence—why we were made— it compels us with a commission—what are we to do while we exist. If I walked into your room and you asked me, "Why are you here?" You wouldn't be asking why I exist, you would be asking me what I came into the room to do. When you ask the big WHY question, both our existence and commission come into play.

To my theologically trained readers who have studied the "why we exist" questions before, their first thoughts may move to the tried and true Westminster Shorter Catechism: "The chief end of man is to glorify God and enjoy him forever." And to my friends who are fond of John Piper's work and refer- ences to Christian Hedonism, they enjoy his revision: "The chief end of man is to glorify God by enjoying him forever."

But let me propose that even these wonderful statements of meaning and purpose are built upon another idea—one more basic and less religious sounding.

God made us to love and for us to love him back. God

made us to be loved by him and for us to reciprocate.

The Baltimore Catechism makes a similar statement: "God made me to know Him, to love Him, and to serve Him in this world, and to be happy with Him forever in heaven."

Scripture doesn't say God made us because he was lonely or bored—even though he is referred to as the one and only God. He didn't need a family or friend—even though he is referred to in scripture as father and friend. Scripture says (Rev 4:11) that everything, the universe and us, was made because it simply gave God pleasure. God made it all because he just wanted to.

You might ask, "Why did he want to?" Well, good luck with this question. It has been asked and unanswered by myriads of thinkers from Socrates to Confucius, from Job to Martin Luther—and it remains unanswered.

But in all seriousness and intellectual honesty, the question reminds me of asking my father the why questions.

"Father, why did you make the universe?"

"Well, little thinker, I made it because I wanted to."

"Why?"

"Ok, little intellectual, let me try and make this simple. Just as an artist wants to create, I wanted to create—so I created. And an artist knows the work he does is so personal that a little piece of himself is seen in all his creations. The art stands on its own, but it can't help but say something about its creator. Anyone who cares to study the art eventually sees the artist himself. It glorifies the artist in this way— it tells you about him, it gives him merit, it honors him."

"Why did you make me?"

"Well, little philosopher, when an artist completes a work and is extremely satisfied with it, as I was when making you, he can't help but love what he made. He holds it in great value, he cares for it. I made you because I'm an artist and I wanted to, so I did. And because I made you, I love you."

"Why?"

"Ok, little skeptic, you're just going to have to trust me on this. Believe me because I tell you. I made you because I wanted to, and I love you because I made you."

Why did God want to create everything? I'm afraid we don't know—he doesn't tell us. But one thing we do know, one thing among many is that God loves us. He told us when he made clothes for Adam and Eve and the promises he gave Abraham, by forgiving David's murder and granting Solomon's request to be a wise leader, for sparing Daniel and his friends when taken into captivity, to Jesus explaining, "For God loved the world so much, he gave..." (John 3:16). Scripture is full of the truth of God's love. He didn't make us to control or manipulate, to have us suffer, or just to sit back and watch. We are no cosmic accident. We were intentionally and wonderfully made for a reason, and because of that we have value and purpose.

OUR OUGHT

What guiding principle comes from this answer to the big WHY question? What does this say about what we ought and ought not do? It's hard to describe, but let me try with another analogy about a good father.

What if you had a great father—a real dad that you knew loved you and wanted the best for you. A man you've watched through the years—and the more you know him, the more you admired him. He has loved you like a good father does—unconditionally—and he straightened you out when you needed it. There were tough times with discipline involved, but all during the tough times you knew deep down that he was doing it for your own good—because he loved you deeply.

How does this make you feel? And, even more importantly, how does this make you act?

I am lucky enough to have such a father. He isn't perfect, but I know he loves me. I know he wants the best for me. He shows it when we talk. He showed me when he came to my football games, my school functions, my knee surgery, my wedding—I could go on.

How does this kind of love affect me? It stirs me to please him. It inspires me to honor him.

We exist, we live, to please and honor God. We love him because he loved us first. When I made mistakes or rebelled, the worst thing I could think of was to have my father know it. Disappointing him would hurt me. Not because I feared his punishment, but because I knew he had high hopes for me.

Knowing that someone you love loves you deeply is very motivating. You want to please and honor them with all your heart. If they tell you to do something, you do it right away. And not only do you do just what they ask, you actually look for additional things you can do for them.

Jesus said, "Whoever has my commands and obeys them, he is the one who loves me." (John 14:21)

John the Apostle said, "We know that we have come to know him if we obey his commands." (1 John 2:3)

SO WHAT?

Why are we here? To love God, and we show it when we desire to please and honor our father in heaven. Not because we have to, but because we want to. We love it. It fulfills us. It charges our soul's batteries.

I think the debate between the Naturals and Spirituals will go on forever—the Naturals and their closed universe, and the Spirituals who have opened up the universe to a heavenly father that exists and has spoken.

The Naturals have their problems. Suppose, out of the blue, scientists discovered another physical dimension, say a tenth dimension, one they can't observe with their eyes but do with their instruments. All they know is that this dimension existed because their instruments noticed something. So this new discovery caused them to speculate that the mysteries of the universe may be hidden in this new dimension (the answers must be there since they can't find them here). Would they ever consider that an intelligence lived in this dimension, an intelligence that affected their own? Possibly, but probably not. Because as soon as they consider it, they would have to consider the ramifications of such an idea—that there may be another someone in another dimension they can't see—a designer, a personality, a God who may have created it all for a reason. He may have created it with a motive and with an end in mind. And if this were true, they would have to conclude that there was a why and a guiding principle to their lives. But who would want to speculate that far. Let's just stay with what we can touch and see.

The Spirituals on the other hand have their own problems. Even though they are favorable to the idea of an open universe and the influence of a creator who has spoken, they have to live consistently with this world view as well. And through the centuries, they have not done a very good job of it.

Do the Naturals have all the answers? Do the Spirituals? Do I have all the answers? No.

Science and knowledge expands and morphs. World economies disappear and societies change. But as all these move forward in time, there are some principles that don't change. I believe there is still black and white, right and wrong, ought and ought not in this world, but there is also a whole lot of gray.

So I'm going to keep on pestering my heavenly father with my questions until I die. I don't think he's grown impatient with me yet.

I'll keep asking why and searching honestly, because we should never fear the truth.

Why are we here? Because out of his artistic inspiration, God placed us here to love, and we can't help but respond by loving him back and living to please and honor him.

"For by Him were all things created that are in heaven and that are on earth, visible and invisible, whether they be thrones or dominions or principalities or powers: all things were created by Him and for Him." (Colossians 1:16)

4
Why Do We Work?
Food, Happiness or Meaning

"Happiness is the meaning and the purpose of life, the whole aim and end of human existence." Aristotle, Greek Philosopher, student of Plato, and tutor to Alexander the Great

"There is no fun like work." Dr. Charles Mayo, founder of the Mayo Clinic

"Go then, eat your bread in happiness and drink your wine with a cheerful heart; for God has already approved your works." (Ecclesiastes 9:7) Solomon, King of Israel in 10th century B.C., philosopher, and one of the wealthiest men who ever lived.

"Beer is proof that God loves us and wants us to be happy." Benjamin Franklin, Scientist, Inventor, Politician and early American Statesmen

HAPPINESS

Do you know the key to happiness?

When I teach classes on Godliness and the workplace, I enjoy opening with such a question.

After receiving a few shy attempts at an answer, I like throwing them a curve.

The key to happiness?

Low expectations.

The class grows quiet for a second. And the first responders slowly react with strange looks and muffled laughter. Then I receive pushback from my type-A students who state with some confused indignation that we shouldn't have low expectations at all. "Our expectations should always be high. We should be confident in everything we do." Having low expectations shows a lack of faith in a God who makes all things work out for good—a God of perpetual positive outcomes (at least from their perspective).

But they miss the point. I'm not talking about faith and Godly plans, I'm talking about the strange, fickle emotion we call happiness. Sometimes we're happy, sometimes we're sad and other times we're stuck in a pleasant neutral. But the force that drives the pendulum from one extreme to the other, from happy to sad, is our expectations.

When a young bride receives flowers from her husband on their anniversary, she beams with happiness. But feel her emotions dive when she later hears from a friend that her prince-charming-of-a-husband had to be reminded that it was their special day, and he just ran into the local Walmart on the way home. What happened? The fact that she received flowers didn't change. Evidently she wasn't expecting the flowers, and her expectations were exceeded—causing "happiness."

Another example comes from the game of golf. Enjoying God's creation while searching the woods for a little white ball defines fun for some of us. Even though I'm not very good, I still enjoy the game. I've played golf with guys who are much better than me, and for some strange reason they don't appear to enjoy it at all. After taking the most relaxed swing, hitting the ball crisply and watching it draw slightly to the left and land within 20 feet of the pin (a shot I would die for), are they happy? No! They shove their club back into the bag and grumble that they didn't follow through correctly, they didn't relax their grip, or some other nonsense.

I then step up to the tee, take my staggered swing, scald the ball with the edge of my iron, and it miraculously lands on the edge of the green, 60 feet from the pin. I'm happy just to be on the green and putting!

I know there are people out there who understand what I'm saying. They've been around the block a time or ten and understand the fickle nature of happiness. Like me, they've been ecstatic with a surprising outcome—"my daughter made the winning shot!"—but they've also been hurt by those they've looked up to (those with whom they had high expectations). We don't want to raise our expectations for fear of being disappointed again. Fool me once, shame on you. Fool me twice, shame on me.

Don't' get me wrong, we definitely enjoy happiness when it comes our way; we just don't hang our heavenly hats on it. Happiness is so temporal, especially when compared to the important things, the things which fulfill and bring meaning to life.

What does this have to do with the reasons why we work? Well, we work to meet our physical needs and the needs of our family, and we may work to pay off the debt created by meeting the needs of our family (I owe, I owe, so off to work I go), however few would say their basic reason for working is to buy basic necessities. They have moved up the ladder of Maslow's Hierarchy of Needs, past the need for food, because their job has allowed them to feed themselves and the family. They have moved past the safety needs by living in a civil society, and arrived at the more spiritual needs of love, esteem and self-actualization.

In today's world where our basic necessities are usually met, I hear the biggest reason for working, or to do anything for that matter, is to be happy.

As we move forward, I would like to put the reasons why we work into four categories. Some people Work to Live It Up (to live life to the fullest—to be happy) while others Live to Work hard and be productive. And then there are those who Work to Evangelize and those who Work as a Commission. The first two are usually related to the Naturals family and the last two are most definitely Spirituals.

WORK TO LIVE IT UP

Life is short.

Ergo, we should take advantage of every second and live life to the fullest. In fact, considering the age of the universe, we are just a blink of an eye.

"All we are is dust in the wind."

"I just have this one life and this one body..."

"The days are long but the years are short."

"Be happy while you're living, for you are a long time dead."

I could go on and on with short pithy sayings about our short life in light of eminent death (a happy thought), but that's how many of us live. Why not? If you knew you only had a few fleeting years and then you're gone, wouldn't you? The old saying, "He who dies with the most toys—wins," makes perfect sense if you compete in business with the short life view, the Work to Live It Up philosophy.

Solomon wrote about this view of life, and Isaiah referred to it back in biblical times (even though they weren't proponents of it). "Eat, drink and be merry, for tomorrow we die." The ancient Roman author Horace coined the phrase, "Carpe diem," or "seize the day," with the same idea in mind—life is short, so get as much of what you want as fast as you can.

Around 350 B.C., the Greek philosopher Epicurus took this "life is short" idea to a whole new level. We have a name for it—Epicureanism. His philosophy has survived the centuries, currently thought of as refined taste and the pursuit of pleasure or happiness. It is to live the high life of satisfaction—whatever makes us happy. In fact Epicurus and his disciples developed a complete system of morality based on their ideas. According to their philosophy, what was right was what made us happy and gave pleasure, and what as wrong was just the opposite, what made us unhappy or brought us pain. To Epicurus, everyone pursuing their own pleasure would eventually equate to one big happy society. His motto was, "Maximize pleasure and minimize pain."

So far, I'm in. Sign me up! Who wouldn't agree with this? Who in their right mind enjoys pain?

But the realities of life, like pebbles in your shoe on a long walk, eventually spoil all the fun. We may work for our happiness, but work is just that—work. And as the thing we do eight hours a day, five days a week becomes more monotonous and less satisfying, eventually we come to see our work not as a form of happiness, but as a means to an end (with the end as our own pleasure), as opposed to work as a satisfying end in itself. And as our work grows less satisfying, morale and motivation wane, and our reason for working shifts away from doing good work for our company to doing as little as we can get away with so we can get as far away from work as we can and on to real life. Or if you are an employer, your attitude would be to get as much out of your slaves (I mean employees) as you can in order to feed your lifestyle of pleasures.

When your view of life is short and there is no lasting or higher purpose, what else do you work for besides pleasure?

Before Epicurus was born, Solomon, a man known for his wealth and wisdom, new the ultimate end of a short life in pursuit of happiness. "He who loves pleasure will become poor; whoever loves luxury will never be rich." (Proverbs 21:17)

The problem with the Work to Live It Up perspective is not that pleasure is a bad thing. The problem is that it is ultimately a very selfish thing, "It's all about me and mine—my happiness, my pleasure"—and selfishness is ultimately unfulfilling and unhappy.

LIVE TO WORK

In the next category are those who Live to Work.

In a way they are like the Epicureans who love pleasure,

but unlike the Epicureans they feel a duty to their fellow man. They are obviously less selfish, but they are equally short sited. They are the Utilitarians.

Jeremy Bentham, a Utilitarian philosopher, stated that nature has placed mankind under two sovereign masters, pain and pleasure. Then, from that moral insight, he derived the Rule of Utility, the "greatest happiness principle".

Similar to Epicureanism, the goal is happiness, but the Utilitiarians define happiness and morality from a different point of view. Their motto is, "The greatest good for the greatest number of people" (with good meaning the greatest happiness and pleasure).

On first reading, the Utilitarian idea has a better ring to it than the Epicurean. At least it takes into consideration the happiness of others and extols the sacrifice of individual pleasures for the pleasure of the community. Wouldn't you be willing to sacrifice a few of your pleasures for the benefit of others? You pay taxes to support our common government. You may give up your family vacation to a co-worker who needs time off for a death in the family. You may even lie to your boss instead of telling him a majority of employees are taking two hour lunch breaks. It's all about doing what is best for the most number of people, right? We will enjoy lunch.

But wait! Just because something is enjoyed by the largest group doesn't make it right. There are some things that are right and wrong no matter how popular they are.

So the spoiler of realism comes around again. Like weeds in a garden, the seeds of the Utilitiarian idea begin to grow, and the fruit begins to reveal itself.

When the group is valued over the individual, the first seed to grow is the loss of individuality. Sure, the sacrifice of self for the community is admirable and altruistic, but taken to its logical end when individuality is shoved aside, eventually we become part of the uncaring machine, just one of many unthinking and uncaring bricks in the wall.

The second seed to grow deals with morality. If what is good is defined by "that which benefits the most people," then it's the majority that decides what is moral. Without any outside guiding principles steering their decisions, whatever the majority decides, no matter how insignificant or harsh, becomes what is right and good for everyone—even for the minority who may disagree. What initially appears altruistic contains the seeds of tyranny. When good is only defined by the greatest number of people, it confirms the Utilitarian ideals and unintended consequences may follow.

But when are theft, or racism, or the suppression of new ideas for that matter, ever really good? If racists were the majority in government, could they pass a law to imprison an entire race and sentence them to forced labor? Coming from the South, this hits too close to home.

If sacrificing an individual's rights for the community is unquestioned with no higher principles of right or wrong, the will of the community can grow to the loss of an individual's rights, or to the discrimination or extinguishing of a minority group altogether.

The problem with Utilitarianism is that it ultimately boils down to losing individual worth and the real possibility of a tyranny of the majority.

VIEWS OF LIFE

The problem isn't necessarily with the Epicurean or Utilitarian views of work—whether you value the individual or the community more highly. Both have their positives and the potential for large negatives. The problem is their view of life. Just as the Naturals and the Spirituals have differing views about the origins and meaning of life, both these groups together see life as short—ending with nothing beyond it.

But life is not short. Life is long.

Life is eternal in fact, and that changes everything.

I won't argue that our days on earth are short—that's true. But life is more than our averaged 74 year life span. This view of life is the major difference between seeing our work as a pursuit of individual or communal pleasure and seeing our work as something with lasting significance.

John Paul Sartre, the French existential philosopher (and not someone who would call himself a spiritual person), probably summed it up as well as any theologian. He said, nothing has real meaning "unless it has an infinite reference point." Unless our lives and work are connected to something that will live beyond us, both will vanish into the void—so they are ultimately insignificant. We may as well live our short lives in whatever manner we wish. All we have is the vain hope that we have affected our world for good before we leave it—however you define good.

Solomon couldn't have said it better. Meaning has nothing to do with our pleasure or our happiness. It has everything to do with eternity. The desire for meaning lies deep within every human heart.

"He (God) has put eternity in the heart of man..." (Ecclesiastes 3:11)

KNOWING AND DOING

I would like to offer a corollary to the original statement about happiness, and with it propose an alternative reason for our work. Its view of life is long (infinite), and its view of existence is that we have been placed on this earth for a reason.

And since this idea is rather complicated, stay with me, it takes a little time to explain.

Yes, the key to happiness is low expectations...

But, the key to meaning is knowing and doing what God wants you to do.

Knowing what God wants and then actually doing it brings fulfillment and meaning precisely because it has an infinite reference point—it won't vanish into the void. It is connected to eternity.

Jesus, after a long day of teaching, and when asked if he was hungry, responded, "My food is to do the will of my Father." Knowing what God wanted him to do, and then doing it, fed his soul like nothing else, it charged his batteries, and it charges ours.

William Wilberforce was a disenchanted politician who desired to leave his corrupt profession and go into the ministry. But John Newton, a friend and converted slave owner, implored him to stay saying, "It's hoped and believed that the Lord has raised you up for the good of the nation." Then after much prayer and consideration, Wilberforce concluded Newton was right. "My business is in the world; and I must mix in the assemblies of men, or quit the post which God seems to have assigned me." And with his time in Parliament, Wilberforce managed to abolish slavery in England.

There is nothing like knowing what God wants you to do and then doing it.

FINDING WHAT GOD WANTS

So, if you accept my premise, your next question is an important one. If the equation is: Eternal meaning and fulfillment equals knowing and doing God's will, then what in the world does God wants us to do?" How do we find that?

In his letter to the Romans, Paul gives insight on how we find what God wants. He concludes, "Then you will be able to test and approve what God's will is—his good, pleasing and perfect will." (Romans 12:2) Evidently there is a way to find it, but it doesn't start with a list of books to read or a list of rules to follow.

The prerequisite for knowing what God wants? It is in

the verse directly before, "... I urge you, brothers, in view of God's mercy, to offer your bodies as living sacrifices, holy and pleasing to God—this is your spiritual act of worship. Do not conform any longer to the pattern of this world, but be transformed by the renewing of your mind. Then you will be able to test and approve what God's will is—his good, pleasing and perfect will." (Romans 12:1-2)

Knowing what God wants doesn't start from a list. It starts with a sacrifice—a change of heart. It starts with a heart that desires to please and honor God.

Read the logical progression in the verses. If you do certain things (first two sentences) you will be able to know what God wants (last sentence).

First give yourself as a "living sacrifice" (this sounds rather gruesome but a living sacrifice is a metaphor for offering your whole life to please and honor God). Then second, and only after you've made such a sacrifice, you go to the next step—you should stop conforming to the patterns of this world (stop acting like the people who don't love God), and renew your mind by filling it up with Godly ideas and not worldly ones.

The first part, offering your life (sacrificing your will), is like an on/off switch—there is no in-between, it's either on or off, offered or taken back. And if you miss the first part there is no need to move forward. There is a spiritual switch that has to be turned on. If you don't turn it on you will only frustrate your life. Trying to understand the will of God without the first part would be like trying to understand British slang without an interpreter—the words sure sound familiar, but you misinterpret them completely.

The second part on the other hand, renewing your mind, is not like an on/off switch. Renewal is ongoing. Renewing your mind takes time. And as your mind is renewed, you will be able to know what God wants of you. It's not all mysterious and mystical, it is time and maturity. The better and longer you know your father God, the easier you'll understand what he wants. So until you have the language down, seek out some interpreters—the counsel of other Godly, mature people.

However, knowing is one thing. As wonderful as it is to understand what God wants, it's quite another to actually do it. Sometimes God's will is rather simple - don't lie, love your wife or children. Other times it pushes us to our limits. But there is nothing more fulfilling.

The Live to Work and Work to Live It Up, Utilitarian and Epicurean ideals for work, both have their positives and negatives, but they fall short in comparison to finding an eternal purpose. But you may be surprised that the Christ following community isn't completely united on their view of work either. Some are convinced that our life's work is to evangelize the world first and foremost, while others are equally convinced that we should be more passive with our words and serve those in need. There are those who Work to Evangelize (like many missionaries) to present Christ to the world, and there are others who Work as a Commission, to serve obvious spiritual and materials needs.

5

Why Should We Work?
The *Other* Great Commission

"How many missionaries does it take to change a light bulb? 101. One to change it and 100 to convince everyone else to change light bulbs too." Anonymous (for a reason— otherwise they would live under threat of missionary harassment)

"Fewer things are harder to put up with than the annoyance of a good example." Mark Twain, aka Samuel L. Clemens, 19th century writer and humorist

"In nothing has the Church so lost her hold on reality as in her failure to understand and respect the secular vocation. She has allowed work and religion to become separate departments, and is astonished to find that, as a result, the secular work of the world is turned to purely selfish and destructive ends, and that the greater part of the world's intelligent workers have become irreligious, or at least, uninterested in religion. But is it astonishing? How can anyone remain interested in a religion which seems to have no concern with nine-tenths of his life?" Dorothy Sayers, an author and professor in England. In April 1942, she delivered an address at Eastbourne, England, entitled, "Why Work?"

HEROES

Back in college, the architecture school was filled with professors of differing philosophies, genders and sexual persuasions, but all of them were inspired by a similar passion—

the art and architecture of the day. These evangelists were constantly exposing us to beautifully photographed buildings, showcasing those architects who were on the cutting edge, the difference makers, the headliners. These guys were our professor's heroes, and ultimately became ours, and by the time we graduated, our image of what architecture was all about was molded by these guys.

However, after graduating and working several years in the field, my eyes were opened to the other world in my profession. The world of architecture was just a small piece in the universe of building. The exposure I received in my years of architecture school were valuable yes, but they only gave me a narrow view of what the profession was all about. My professors didn't expose me completely to the world I would find myself in. Instead they focused on what they were passionate about—their heroes. They had no ill motive or deception in mind. They just wanted to share what inspired them.

I can't help but say this is the case in many churches. Our pastors and priests have their own heroes who inspire them. They've studied them in seminary, read of them in books and follow their lives—and hope their lives affect ours. Why wouldn't our pastors and priests want to inspire us with the same people who inspire them?

But just as the world of architecture is vast in comparison to my view of it from college, the world of Godly work is larger than what is standard presentation in our churches.

There is no conspiracy here—no one trying to deceitfully manipulate us. It's just an innocent blind spot in the loving hearts of our spiritual leaders. However, the unintended consequence is the subtle demeaning of the work most of the congregation chooses to do. It's implied that their work is not as valuable as the sacred work of the church. It's never stated because it's never considered. But what is presented as important on Sunday creates a disconnect between the work of the church and the lives of a majority of the congregation—a disconnect between the spiritual world and the material world.

If you go to modern and evangelical churches these days and ask, "What we are supposed to be doing in this lifetime—during our working days?" From these churches, para-churches or other spiritual organizations you'll most likely hear, "to seek and save the lost," or to "go and make disciples." In essence, our emphasis should be to go make or find other Christians—not to do good work for our employer. Every Sunday, the sermon, homily and the songs we sing all revolve around this purpose—the evangelical mission.

"Therefore go and make disciples of all nations, baptizing them in the name of the Father and of the Son and of the Holy Spirit, and teaching them to obey everything I have commanded you..."(Matthew 28:19-20)

Don't misinterpret my intensions here. My aim is not to bring down the pastor, priest or missionary, it is to raise up the good and Godly work of the plumber, architect and lawyer to the noble and respectable calling it is.

WORK TO EVANGELIZE

Some evangelistic-minded pastors and priests have recognized the disconnect between the work of the church and the work days of their congregants, so when teaching on the significance of work, their answer is a logical progression of their own calling—for us to be like them, to be missionaries, but in the workplace. Our workplace is our mission field, and the reason for all work remains the same, to make or find other Christians. The only difference is the location it takes place, not the church or a foreign country, but at work.

For evangelically minded workers, your main mission is to go to work every morning thinking, "Who can I talk to about Christ today?" You pray and look forward to guiding conversations to spiritual matters and the gospel of Christ. Our work (our plumbing, teaching or carpentering) is mainly a platform for sharing, with a secondary purpose to meet our needs. Are we called to spend 40 or more hours of our week working the mission field of commerce? Many say, "yes" and I don't disagree.

A pastor told of a young man who came to him after being fired from his job claiming he was persecuted for his faith. His boss had caught him sharing the gospel during work. It just so happened our pastor knew the boss, and out of concern he called him to inquire. The boss then shared how poor a worker the young man was —how he was constantly ignoring the work he was hired to do in order to perform his real work—sharing his faith.

This young man didn't just lose his job, he lost his integrity. Is God pleased when we agree to work hard for our employer and then play hooky while we do God's work?

All this has raised a question in my mind: If our main spiritually sanctioned reason for working is to share our faith, then why does God ask us to spend so much time writing code, teaching math, or putting screws into sheetrock? Is this just part of the investment we make for a spiritual pay off?

For the Work to Evangelize folks, it is a definite yes. And thank God for them because we need people who love to verbalize the gospel of Christ with passion. But for many other personality types there is another God-given motivation for work.

WORK AS A COMMISSION

A widely published businessman, Steven Covey, the author of Seven Habits of Highly Effective People, recommended we should "begin and work with the end in mind." I can't think of better advice to give to young men and women going into the business world. The ultimate end of what you're doing should guide every day of your work—each and every decision.

As an architect, if the end (the aim) of your work is to provide a building for doctors to attend to their patients, then it is a waste of time to research the building code for a gymnasium. If you have a question about how a doctor's office will be used, you don't ask the plumber. Only the doctor and patient know the details of their needs. If you work with the doctor and patient's needs in mind, you remain focused on a building which will meet those needs.

The great commission is a wonderful and Godly end to have in mind when you approach your work, but there is another commission in the Bible. I call it the Other Great Commission. It starts in the beginning where God, the creative artist, mysteriously formed the universe.

"Then God said, 'Let us make man in our image, in our likeness, and let them rule over the fish of the sea and the birds of the air, over the livestock, over all the earth, and over all the creatures that move along the ground.' So God created man in his own image, in the image of God he created him; male and female he created them. God blessed them and said to them, 'Be fruitful and increase in number; fill the earth and subdue it. Rule over the fish of the sea and the birds of the air and over every living creature that moves on the ground.'" (Genesis 1:26-28)

Think about this for a second. Before humans were made, God had a plan, a calling, a commission in mind for us. We were to watch over his creation, and he wrote our job description in four tasks: to be fruitful, to fill the earth, to subdue it, and to rule it.

Notice he gave us this job description, this "work" to do, before any mention of a special fruit, a snake, or the bad choices of Adam and Eve. God worked and gave us work to do. Work is not a punishment, it is a commission. It's one of the reasons he put us here. Work only became hard as a result of the choices Adam made and God giving us the consequences of those choices.

I've wondered if work would have eventually become monotonous if Adam and Eve hadn't fallen? Would our work have been straining and hard as we plowed the ground? Would our animals give us little brown presents to scoop up and fertilize with? Would we have used our God given creativity to make tools—a plow, a combine, a computer—to make life and work more productive? Possibly and possibly not. We don't know. But we do know God had a job in mind when He created us—to join in his work.

Two of the four parts of God's commission are relatively simple—multiply and fill/inhabit the earth. One is to make babies, and the other is not to stay congregated in one spot for too long. The first comes rather naturally. The second is harder since we tend to like hanging around each other (the Tower of Babel took care of some of that).

The other two parts of our commission relate more to our work. God says to "subdue" and "rule over" his creation. To subdue it means to tame or overtake the world (or not have it overtake you), while to rule means to manage it as well as God would—be active in making sure the creation, the world, the animals and ourselves, were well taken care of, as if he were doing the job himself.

WORK IS SPIRITUAL

To the Work as a Commission people, the Gospel, the good news about God, is a little broader than the Work to Evangelize people think of it. It is good meaningful news that God created us with a purpose in mind. It is good news that our daily work has significance because we are doing what God made us for. Teaching children lessons to live in a modern world is Godly and necessary to keep it functioning well. Building buildings for teaching children, or to house other places of commerce, not only provides work and profit for the contractor, it requires resources and work from hundreds of other people, all creating benefit for others—the nail maker, the nail gun manufacturer, the nail gun repair man.

Adam Smith, one of the first economists (using his God-commissioned powers of observation and reasoning), noted how the division of labor and the use of tools had improved the lives of people all over the world. Dividing labor (breaking down a project into smaller, more efficient tasks) has made work more productive. Henry Ford took those ideas and by mastering assembly lines and using tools from the creative minds of men (creative as God is creative), stopped making cars one at a time, and started building them hundreds per day, reducing the cost of the automobile so that even the workers who made them could afford them.

Who wants to kill their own farm animals and process that meat for the evening meal when they can instead go to work, make money from the thing they are trained for, and trade that money for meat that was processed in a sanitized plant? Multiply this idea times billions of jobs and we have the current economy—a complex (some say too complex) system of labor, resources, investment, and creativity which keeps the modern world going. Many would call this part of the Common Grace of God—a world economy which has extended life, cured diseases, fed the world during famine—and the list could go on.

Using our God-given creativity didn't start with Adam Smith. Since a man created and used the first plow to increase a crop yield, God has blessed our creativity, and the world, especially the poor, have benefited.

None of this sounds very spiritual, does it—division of labor, tools, assembly lines? Well, neither does going to work every day. But it should be seen as a very spiritual activity.

Wayne Grudem, in his book *Business for the Glory of God,*

writes, "But how should we remember the poor? How should we open our hearts to our brother in need? A short-term solution is to give food and clothing to the poor, and that is certainly right. But it is no long-term solution, for the food is soon eaten and the clothing wears out."

Grudem said, "I believe the only long-term solution to world poverty is business. That is because businesses produce goods, and businesses produce jobs. And businesses continue producing goods year after year and continue providing jobs and paying wages year after year. Therefore if we are ever going to see long-term solutions to world poverty, I believe it will come through starting and maintaining productive, profitable businesses."

What does writing computer code, teaching middle school students, and constructing buildings have to do with the spiritual life? It is God's commission. What is more spiritual than knowing and doing what God wants?

FULFILLMENT

Then why aren't we fulfilled when writing code if it's what God wants? Why aren't we joyful after a full day of installing pipe?

I believe it's because down deep we think our work has no eternal purpose. We have disconnected our working lives from our spiritual lives.

Are the people who see Work as a Commission saying that by simply doing work we are fulfilling the "will of God?" Yes they are, and because this is what God asks us to do, it gives significance and meaning to our work like nothing else.

"Whatever you do, work at it with all your heart, as working for the Lord, not for men." (Colossians 3:23)

Whether you're a salesman, an engineer, a janitor, a preacher or a priest, whatever you do, do it with your whole heart and give it your best effort as though your boss was God himself. I know plumbers who get it and work this way, and unfortunately there are pastors who don't.

I can already hear the pushback from my friends who see Work to Evangelize as the main reason for our work, but that's all right. There are working men and women reading this for the first time who feel the weight of Mt. Everest removed from their shoulders. For years they have sensed the futility of work and the guilt for not living up to the expectations of their evangelically minded friends.

God has commissioned them to be good rulers of His creation through their work, and by working in a loving and Godly manner, they are performing a noble and Godly commission. They have read Paul telling his Corinthian friends, "... each one should retain the place in life that the Lord assigned to him and to which God has called him. This is the rule I lay down in all the churches. ...Each one should remain in the situation which he was in when God called him." (1 Corinthians 7:17-21)

Some have read all of Paul's letters and wondered why he didn't constantly tell those who didn't share his calling to go seek and save the lost and never repeated the Great Commission stated in Matthew. But Paul did constantly talk about growing in Godliness. If the Great Commission of evangelism, something I truly believe in, was such a universal requirement for everyone, wouldn't it be quoted again somewhere else?

In one of Jesus' early lessons, the Sermon on the Mount, he called those who followed him the salt of the earth, as though Godly people act like a preservative and flavoring for the entire world. He then said they were the light of the world, as though God were shining through them—providing truth, exposing good and evil, and doing the very work of God. Then he ended this lesson with, "Let your light shine before people in such a way that they may see your good works and glorify (give honor and great weight to) God." (Matthew 5:16)

Jesus tells us to do good work—public good work. And may I offer that doing good work for your employer is one of them. It means loving your neighbor by giving to the needy. It means not lying or stealing certainly, but it also means doing a good job at the place you spend most of your time, and the place where others observe your life—your workplace. In fact, your work could actually be the best place to do good works (good work for your employer, good work for your family, good work for others) and have your co-workers observe what God is like because of it.

"We are ambassadors for Christ, as though God were making his appeal through us..." (2 Corinthians 5:20)

I don't presume that an exceptional job at code writing would cause your co-workers to glorify God. A few computer geeks may get excited, but I expect very few others would. The good works Jesus is talking about are those which obviously belong to Godly people, who act like salt and light—sometimes stinging and sometimes enlightening. He's talking about extraordinary things, the extra mile things he talks about later in his sermon, and doing extraordinary things because we really want to, not because we are required to.

You'll be the most obvious person in the office if you live a life of simple but obvious Godliness. You will stand out when you're the one who doesn't get angry or use expletives when something doesn't go your way. You'll turn your boss' head when you tell him (privately and respectfully) you'd rather not do something even slightly unethical. Your friends at work may love to hear the story of your family vacation spent building an orphanage. And everyone will notice when you keep your word, especially if by doing so it costs you something.

If you do these things humbly and to please and honor God they may ask themselves, "What is special about that guy?" They will see how rewarding and joyful a selfless, holy life can be. And they will definitely notice if you meet with them privately and lovingly meet a personal need of theirs.

Your life could be so obviously Godly that you would have to defend your Godly actions. "Why are you so kind, or honest, or truthful?"

"For we are God's workmanship, created in Christ Jesus to do good works, which God prepared in advance for us to do." (Ephesians 2:8-10)

OFFENSIVE AND DEFENSIVE LIVING

The Apostle Peter said, "Always be prepared to give a defense to everyone who asks you to give the reason for the hope that you have. But do this with gentleness and respect." (1 Peter 3:15)

In many ways it would be better to defend your extraordinary good work than to make a quick proposal about your faith to someone who doesn't know you. Sometimes we should earn the right to discuss our faith before diving into something so personal. Isn't that better than telling someone about the life you love, when they haven't seen it lived out first?

"Preach the gospel at all times. If necessary, use words," St Francis of Assisi said.

Those who lean toward the Work to Evangelize world, tend to be on the offensive (go and tell), while others tend to be defensive minded (live it and be ready to explain it), but both are encouraged to communicate the reason for their faith when it's time to do so. Paul and Peter appear to be defensive minded when it comes to our relationships with those outside our faith, but I sense they taught an assertive defense.

I love the church. And when I say the church, I'm not necessarily talking about the organized Church. I'm referring to the body of believers who humbly trust in Christ and follow his teaching—loving God with all their heart and loving their neighbor as themselves. But I have some concerns, particularly with the evangelical church, a group with whom I've been deeply involved, in many roles over 35 years—a church in which I still to lead.

My concern is not the current tendency toward Christian consumerism—coming to church to get a free cup of coffee, meet with a few spiritually minded associates, hear a good talk and then go back to life. Motives are mixed and change, and people mature as they are exposed to the truth at a good church, so let the consumers keep coming.

It's not the politicization of the Christian worldview as Republican, Democratic, Socialist or whatever. Nor is it the creation of political action committees and lobbyists pushing religious causes. Thank God we have the opportunity to express our thoughts and concerns to those who govern.

And it's not the use of economic principals, creating mega-churches whose seeker-friendly models appeal to a materialistic world. These huge churches meet the needs of thousands and affect large cities for Godliness. I say use every tool at your disposal—be shrewd and innocent as Jesus suggested.

The concern I have is the bent toward over-spiritualizing. In recent years if we, the church, communicate anything of importance it must be couched in god-words with spiritual overtones—a version of Christian political correctness.

What God wants from us is not always mystical or super natural, but reasonable and obvious to everyone. The over-spiritualizing I refer to focuses on our special, extra-personal relationship with God (I am emphasizing "personal" to the point of being narcissistic - everything that happens relates to me, it's about maturing me, humbling me, praying for me).

I need to walk carefully here because I don't want to be misunderstood. Scripture says God loves each one of us and does have a wonderful plan for our lives. We do seek a personal special relationship with the God our father, but after that we are to take the focus off of ourselves and point it toward others.

We have a generation of young people (college graduates) who sit, confused, waiting for a mystical calling from God for the ultimate purpose for their working lives. They pray and pray, seek Godly counsel who also prays for God's perfect will, and when given reasonable and good advice, they wonder whether it is of God since they haven't felt a true call—an emotional tug. All the while there's a job out there ready for them to use their talents and education, where they can add value to God's creation by feeding their families and serving others—being involved in the world of commerce.

Am I saying don't make big plans or prayerfully seek God's guidance? No, but I am speaking from experience and the knowledge that occupations and commitments change over life's span, and very few people receive a life long calling in the world of business or ministry. I know 60 year olds looking back over their lives who laughingly ask, "I wonder what God wants me to do when I grow up?

THE GREAT COMMANDMENT TEAM

We are on the same team—those who Work to Evangelize and Work as a Commission. One plays offense and the other plays defense, but we're both on the same team. When we work together everything falls into place—our commission from God and the knowledge, skills and experiences we offer.

We work because we love God, and we show it by doing what he asks of us and telling others about it. We also work to love our neighbors—our actual neighbors, but also our co-workers, our bosses and employees—everyone in our sphere of influence. He asks us to take care of the creation he made by meeting the physical and spiritual needs that exist and we do so by being active in commerce and people's lives, doing extraordinarily good work and being prepared to give a defense for our actions through kind and honest words.

I once served on a leadership board with a man who has become a good friend of mine—an entrepreneur in the renewable energy business. This man was married later in life to woman who had been on staff with Campus Crusade for Christ for many years. He told me of one of their early marital conversations (I'll paraphrase).

"My love," said his wife, "your time discipling and evangelizing is more important than your time finding and selling energy. When are you going to spend more time doing what counts for eternity—God's work?"

"Love of my life," my friend responded, "we support our church and five missionaries right now, and I sense God has me right where he wants me—In the world of business and energy. If I were to spend more time doing what you call God's work, we may have to stop supporting the missionaries. But if I continue with my business, and God blesses it, we may be able to support another one hundred missionaries. What would be better?"

Although I believe our work is much more than a funding mechanism for ministry, my friend has a point. We're on the same team. We need my friend's wife and we need my friend's work to do what God made all humans to do—take care of his creation, the world and its people, by meeting their physical and spiritual needs.

6

Business vs. Godliness

"Obviously crime pays, or there'd be no crime." G. Gordon Liddy, mastermind of the Watergate break-in that sent him to prison and precipitated the resignation of President Richard Nixon

"Of the billionaires I've known, money just brings out the basic traits in them. If they were jerks before they had money, they are simply jerks with a billion dollars." Warren Buffett, Investor, and the world's 2nd wealthiest person (2009)

"In terms of allocation of time resources, religion is not very efficient. There's a lot more I could be doing on Sunday morning." Bill Gates, founder of Microsoft, and the world's wealthiest person (1995-2009)

"To work is to pray." St. Benedict of Nursia, from the Rule of St. Benedict and his thoughts on work and prayer, 7th century

"No one can serve two masters. Either he will hate the one and love the other, or he will be devoted to the one and despise the other. You cannot serve both God and Money." (Matthew 6:24) Jesus, from the Sermon on the Mount

THE GREAT CONUNDRUM

Evidently there's a problem between God and the almighty dollar. As Jesus said, "You cannot serve God and money." It appears you are either on God's side, devoted to him and despising money, or you're on money's side, hating God and loving money—there is no in-between.

But someone tell me—what's wrong with money? And how does anyone serve it? Money is just a piece of paper, a thing—although a very useful thing. Even our pastors and priests work for a paycheck every day (money) to pay their bills. Are they serving money? There has to be something deeper, something within the very nature of moneymaking that opposes the nature of God and Godliness. Otherwise I don't think Jesus would have been so emphatic about it.

And of imminent value to the remainder of this book, if we can't reconcile the problems between God and money we might as well give up—and you might as well stop reading right now. If business is all about making money, then according to Jesus it is an ungodly pursuit and should be abandoned immediately. If money and God are by nature in conflict, we all might as well quit our jobs and become monks or itinerant preachers.

THE NATURE OF THINGS

To a hammer, the whole world is a nail.

Use your cartoon imagination and think of yourself as a hammer—a round wooden stick with a metal head on one end. How do you define your world? What were you made to do? Why do you exist? To hammer nails, of course. It's in your nature.

To a mathematician or physicist the world is an equation. These guys define their world in mathematic terms—it's the way they understand it. Einstein's simple formula $E=MC^2$ redefined the nature of the physical universe for these guys causing an explosion of additional equations for nuclear energy and space-time relationships.

What does the world look like to a person in the business world? A factory? A dollar bill? What is the nature of business?

If you've taken even a basic course in economics, you

know the world of business is not simple—multinational corporations, banks making loans to manufacture cars or medicine in foreign countries, governments regulating currency, congressmen creating laws restricting trade or levying taxes to manipulate commerce, billions of people and trillions of dollars changing hands. Saying the world of business is complex is an understatement.

But when you talk about the nature of something, you look past its complexities. You break it down to its core elements—its essence. When you look at steam, water and ice, they appear very different, but at their core, in their nature they are just water. The whole world of business is almost incomprehensible, but the nature of business is very simple.

BUSINESS

For most people their only reference to business is their job. They go to work each day, trade their time, education, and experience for a paycheck, go home, pay the rent, and eat with their friends or family. They seldom think of the person who created their job—the one who saw a need, put a business plan together, hired employees, bought equipment and started the money machine running. Your job is a big part of business, but your job and the work you do are not the nature of business.

There are those who would say the very nature of business is profit and greed—a morally wrong enterprise—taking advantage of the less-fortunate or the less-educated for reasons of making lots of money. Unfortunately, I've observed this myself and understand them, but only to a point. Ungodly, ill-gained profit is something God hates (yes God hates certain things), as with the men who deal with inconsistent measurements of grain or other items for trade, for example. "The Lord abhors dishonest scales, but accurate weights are his delight." (Proverbs 11:1)

Making a legitimate profit is not greed. A business that doesn't make a profit has a very limited life. Certainly a business could break even (make no profit) and keep all their employees employed, but when inevitable problems arise (a mistake in manufacturing, an economic downturn, or a lawsuit or two), or if the stability of the company requires money for research and development, unless there is a profit pool to dip into, the business may fail. Not all profit is greed, it's a guard against mistakes and an investment in sustainability.

Unfortunately, to many businessmen the bottom line is profit only, and they'll cut moral corners to get it. Back in 2001, Nike made the headlines with an article stating, "The multibillion dollar sportswear company Nike admitted yesterday that it 'blew it' by employing children in third world countries, but added that ending the practice might be difficult." Nike admitted their moral failure and made changes.

Hiring children, after most industrialized nations have passed child labor laws, grates against our modern moral senses. We envision large steamy factories with sweaty little kids laboring under the threat of a beating. There is obviously a problem here—a moral problem.

But child labor laws have possible unintended consequences. In some countries, keeping children from working would be harmful to their family. Some societies rely on everyone working just to survive—with children as an economic resource and education a luxury they can't afford.

These moral issues are not always as black and white as they first appear. A company manufacturing sportswear is neither right or wrong, moral or immoral. The company and the things they produce, cloth or shoes, are neither moral or immoral - they are just things.

Similarly, a drug is just a thing, but the making and distributing of narcotics can be both moral or immoral depending on the narcotic being manufactured and the nature for dispensing it. A doctor can prescribe morphine to a patient in pain, but a drug pusher would break the law if he purchased or sold it himself. A drug like morphine is just a thing made by a pharmaceutical company. The action of placing a drug into a syringe and injecting it into a person is neither good nor evil either. It is the motive (the heart) behind the action that moves the injection into the realm of good or bad, moral or immoral. Doctors prescribe it for good and pushers sell it for evil. It is the intent, the motive, the heart behind the use of a thing that moves it to the realm of morality.

But I'm getting ahead of myself regarding morality. Let's stay with the nature of business.

SIMPLE TRADE

From the largest multinational conglomerate to the smallest local mom and pop store, businesses have one thing in common—the same thing modern day companies have in common with every company that existed before them. Business boils down to one person exchanging something they have with another person—a simple trade. That is the nature of business.

Exxon, Firestone, Microsoft, Whole Foods, Time Warner, and lowly authors of books on Godliness in business all depend on the same thing: one person wanting their product, and that same person trading what they have for it—his hard-earned cash for oil, tires, software, food, entertainment, or even a book.

You have actually been in business your entire life— the business of trade. From the time you began to read in elementary school, you were trading your time (although involuntarily) for the skill of reading.

Later as you went through high school, you traded more of your time for math, logic and literary skills which made you useful (and marketable) in the world. If you were able to get into a college, you then traded the money you accumulated (or the money your parents accumulated) for more refined knowledge and skills, and with these higher and more refined skills, you became more and more valuable in the marketplace.

Then with unique skills in hand, you entered the world of commerce. If your educational decisions were good ones, there was a demand for what your skills supplied. You then traded your time and skills for money and in turn, traded that money for rent, food, fun, etc. It's all about trade. You trade what you think is valuable for something someone thinks is valuable. And what you think is valuable is what you value. And how do we determine what you value? From your values, your principles—your morality.

Chick-Fil-A, a company I admire, provides chicken sandwiches, fries and other fast foods, but they have an unusual set of values based on their founder S. Truett Cathy's view of business. While most food franchises stay open on Sunday, they are closed. Mr. Cathy said, "Our decision to close on Sunday was our way of honoring God and directing our attention to things more important than our business. If it took seven days to make a living with a restaurant, then we needed to be in some other line of work. Through the years, I have never wavered from that position."

Chick-Fil-A's values are different than other companies' values who remain open on Sunday. But even with their values and their loyal following, Chick-Fil-A would be forced to close their doors if their food was not what their customers valued and wanted to trade their money for.

Without a trade, the business world would not exist. The nature of business is simple trade.

THE NATURE OF GODLINESS

Just as the nature of business is simple, the nature of Godliness is also simple—or it should be.

Godliness is not a particular religion or a nondescript

spirituality. The definition of Godliness is simply acting in a Godly way. The nature of Godliness is just being Godly—acting like God would act, thinking what God would think, feeling what God would feel. (I didn't say it was easy, I just said it was simple.)

"I am the Lord your God; consecrate yourselves and be holy, because I am holy... I am the Lord who brought you up out of Egypt to be your God; therefore be holy, because I am holy." (Leviticus 11:44-47)

To be holy means to be special, set apart, the way God is set apart, special and unique in character.

"You were taught, with regard to your former way of life, to put off your old self, which is being corrupted by its deceitful desires; to be made new in the attitude of your minds; and to put on the new self, created to be like God in true righteousness and holiness." (Ephesians 4:22-24)

RULES

I find it amazing how difficult people make being holy and Godly (and I say being holy and not acting holy for a reason). They miss such a simple idea and instead create a list of rules to live by (and expectations that everyone else should live by), and then try as hard as they can to follow the rules. They see Godliness as a discipline, not a desire—a regimen to follow and not a delight to be part of. They are as different as Mary and Martha who had Jesus over for dinner.

"As Jesus and his disciples were on their way, he came to a village where a woman named Martha opened her home to him. She had a sister called Mary, who sat at the Lord's feet listening to what he said. But Martha was distracted by all the preparations that had to be made. She came to him and asked, 'Lord, don't you care that my sister has left me to do the work by myself? Tell her to help me!'

"'Martha, Martha,' the Lord answered, 'you are worried

and upset about many things, but only one thing is needed. Mary has chosen what is better, and it will not be taken away from her.'" (Luke 10:38-42)

I don't think Jesus was complaining that Martha didn't appreciate him being there. And I don't think Jesus was praising Mary for sitting around and not helping. It was that Martha got caught up in her own rules and her definition of hospitality and didn't understand the big picture—that he came by their house for another purpose.

Being like God is not a disciplined regimen of do's and don'ts, although when you understand it you will want to do some things and you will not want to do others. Being like God is more than imitating his actions. There's a major heart factor in it.

Although some may call me an artist, I am not. I tinker at it and understand it, but I wouldn't call myself an artist. My father, brothers and daughter on the other hand are real artists. It's in their nature—their DNA. It's an expression of who they are.

Now if I wanted to be like my father, who is a landscape painter, I could gather originals of all his work and start copying them. After years of this I could become the most amazingly disciplined copier of his work and probably get pretty proficient at painting the things he does. I may learn his technique and pallet of colors. But I can only touch the surface of really knowing my father by copying his paintings.

If someone asked me to go find something my father loved and then paint it, all I could do is look at what he painted in the past and copy it again. That's as far as I can go. I may know how and what he painted, but I wouldn't know what he loved to paint.

To know what my father loved, I would have to get to know him, not just copy his work or actions. He would have to share with me his inner longings, his disappointments, his joys, and the things he loves. Only then could I know the heart of my father and become a painter like him.

If all you do is imitate God's behavior and don't under-stand his heart (the things he loves and delights in), you'll be an empty, repetitive copy—trying, trying and failing, instead of a unique individual searching and finding the nature, the heart, of God.

BEING LIKE GOD

Then what is the nature and heart of God? In what way can we know and actually be like him? Obviously we have a few limitations—especially with the whole omniscience and omnipresence thing. But I don't think that's what scripture means when it says, be like God. It means to understand and know his heart.

"This is what the Lord says: 'Let not the wise man boast of his wisdom or the strong man boast of his strength or the rich man boast of his riches, but let him who boasts boast about this: that he understands and knows me, that I am the Lord, who exercises kindness, justice and righteousness on earth, for in these I delight,' declares the Lord." (Jeremiah 9:23-24)

This is one of my favorite verses in scripture. It inspires me. For someone who has reached what some call a level of success in life and business, it secures my foundation onto what is real and true.

Who can say they've gained any wisdom, strength, or riches on their own?

Well, to be perfectly honest, we did have something to do with it. We've studied hard in school and learned hard lessons from our experiences, and we've gained a bit of wis-dom. We've worked out and strengthened our bodies. We may even say we've worked hard, took some risks and gained a certain amount of wealth. But can we actually take credit for of it? Not really.

There were myriads of concurrent events that have lead to any success we've had—friends, friends of friends, coworkers, economic boons and busts—all working together with the reality of God's hand in it. You can't take complete credit for any success really. Who can ever really boast?

But there is one thing we can boast about, and it's like boasting about your family. I'm extremely proud to be the son of truth seeking parents and the brother of wonderful brothers and sisters. I know them. I understand them. And I'm proud of them. They make me look good just by being in their family. But how much more is it to be proud of our heavenly father and boast about knowing and understanding him?

But this is just the beginning of the verse. When we get to the conclusion, God shares what he loves and does—and not only this, but what he absolutely delights in.

God delights in kindness, justice, and righteousness. What human being on earth wouldn't want to be like this?

KIND, JUST AND RIGHTEOUS

It's from these three attributes that we get a glimpse into the heart of God—why he does what he does. These three attributes balanced, combined together, and used with skill describe what God is like. Taken separately they don't tell the whole story. Separately they become a caricature of who God is. These three attributes are like a three legged stool— take away one leg and it falls.

Take kindness for example. Who would ever object to being kind? It's a form of love that exudes Godliness—a form of mercy, the heart of compassion for those in need, the ability to forgive when someone offends you. Yet it's possible to be kind at the wrong time and to the wrong person. Would you tell the murderer running toward our child, "Pardon me, kind sir, please don't run toward my child with that knife."

No. It would be righteous and just not to be kind. In fact, it would be kind (to your child)—it would be right and just to stop him before he gets anywhere near to them.

Without justice and righteousness, kindness becomes a wishy-washy, aimless, can't-we-all-just-get-along, caricature of who God is. Kindness needs to be balanced and stable to be Godly. Kindness is an extension of love, but real love, tough mature love, requires the other two traits righteousness and justice. When balanced you can be kind to anyone—even love your enemies by having compassion for them but still protecting those you are responsible for.

Justice on its own has similar problems. When you desire justice without balancing it with kindness or righteousness you tend to become revengeful. Without kindness and righteousness you might feel justified to hit the person who ran into your car at an intersection. What's holding you back? "That idiotic teenager was talking on their cell, ran the stop sign and hit me! He or she deserves just punishment." In fact, since all you're after is justice, you should take your car and ram theirs' a few times to make things equal.

Righteousness has its problems too. We all know people who walk around with a holier-than-thou attitude. These guys can quote a scripture for everything they see you doing wrong. These legalists are anything but kind and the only justice they see is punishment for anyone not meeting their standards.

Righteousness needs kindness and justice to balance out its legalistic tendencies. Justice needs righteousness and kindness to avoid revenge. And kindness needs to be doled out in a just and right manner, otherwise the dispenser of kindness may get run over completely. God is completely righteous. No one can accuse him. He is completely just. No one can question his knowledge and wisdom. And he is completely kind. No one loves or sacrifices as he does. Sometimes you should do what is right; sometimes you should do what is just; and sometimes you should be kind. And I don't think it's a coincidence that the first attribute ascribed to God in the verse is kindness. I believe in a majority of instances, or when in doubt, we should be kind first.

Kindness, justice and righteousness, this is the heart of God.

GRACE

There is another characteristic of God that goes to his nature. It's called Grace.

The term Grace in scripture is very different than the one commonly used. We say a dancer has grace, or we assign the term grace to a host at a party, "You were a gracious host." (not meaning they dance all that well, but that they were hospitable). But the term grace when assigned to God has a very different meaning and it's often confused with kindness and mercy.

Mercy is defined as *not* receiving what you *do* deserve.

God is merciful, and I'm glad of it. When I mess up, I deserve the consequences of my actions. If I lie or steal I deserve the shame, distrust and penalty that follows, but God sometimes shows me mercy. When I receive mercy, I do not receive what I deserve.

But Grace is something very different. Grace is *receiving* something you *don't* deserve. It's an unexpected and unearned gift.

It reminds me of a story about a judge, his son, and a friend.

There once was a judge who lived in small town with his teenaged son. Both the judge and his son had a common friend, a young man with hard family problems who tried to drown them away with alcohol. They'd known this young man all his life, and as they observed him fall deeper into his addiction, they grew to love him more—a compassionate, caring love. The son would often go pick his friend up from bars, drive him home and clean the vomit left on the back seat.

One evening the young man decided to drive himself home from a bar, and it wasn't until the judge received a late night call that he knew the young man had driven into a local convenience store, killing a patron. He was soon arrested and tried for his crime.

At the conclusion of the trail where the father presided as judge, the jury found the young man guilty and sentenced to prison.

At the sentencing the judge made his pronouncement. "As the judge in this case, you know I have full jurisdiction and the power to increase or decrease the prison sentence. I know it's unprecedented, but after speaking long and hard to my son, who is a good friend of this young man, we have decided that my son will take this man's place, pay the full penalty for the crime, and his friend will go free."

This is an example of grace—receiving what you do not deserve.

The one thing that distinguishes the life and work of Jesus was his grace. The one thing that distinguishes true Christianity from other religions is grace. If we live the best life we can, die and stand before God, we can always plead for mercy. But we can't plead for grace. Grace is a gift God chooses to give.

"For it is by grace you have been saved, through faith— and this not from yourselves, it is the gift of God—not by works, so that no one can boast." (Ephesians 2:8)

Grace is the gift and choice of God.

LOVE THAT IS NO BURDEN

The heart of God is to be completely kind, fully just, and truly righteous, and like a loving father God has sacrificed and chosen to give us a gift we don't deserve—by granting us grace. And if God is like this, it inspires me to be like him, and to obey him, but not because I have to, because I want to.

The Apostle John, in his first letter to the church, drives home the point about the thankful and inspired hearts of those who want to please and honor him.

"For this is the love of God: to obey his commands. And his commands are not burdensome..." (1 John 5:3)

Have you ever been asked very nicely to do something you weren't qualified for—like asking an artist to do taxes, or an accountant to write music? You probably said yes because they asked so nicely, but deep down inside you knew your heart wasn't in it. It was a burden.

A friend once told of a fellow who approached him on the street asking for money. As one who desires to be Godly, my friend looked the guy over to see if he looked like a drug addict or was legitimately in need. In this particular situation he couldn't tell, and he didn't have time to perform an investigation into the man's life, so he begrudgingly reached into his pocket and gave the man a few dollars.

Asking why he did it, he told me, "I did it because I love God, and I would feel guilty if I hadn't."

He did a good thing for sure, but he did it because he felt like he had to. His heart wasn't in it. It was a burden.

I have news for my friend. Yes, he did a good thing by helping a person in need, but he didn't do it out of full love for God. He didn't do it like God would have done it. If he were to do it as God does it (if he were to love as God loves), he would have wanted to give his money to the man—from a heart of compassion and concern, not of guilt or obligation.

This is the love of God, "to obey his commands. And his commands are not burdensome." The word "and" is extremely important in this verse. The act of loving God is not only doing what he asks, it is doing what he asks with the right motives, the right heart. Doing something with the love of God means it is not a burden—we love doing it.

When discussing giving money to the mission of the

church, the Apostle Paul said, "Each man should give what he has decided in his heart to give, not reluctantly or under compulsion, for God loves a cheerful giver." (2 Corinthians 9:7)

Jesus said, "Come to me, all you who are weary and burdened, and I will give you rest. Take my yoke upon you and learn from me, for I am gentle and humble in heart, and you will find rest for your souls. For my yoke is easy and my burden is light." (Luke 10:28—30)

The love of God, the real love of God when you find it, leads you to do what he asks because you want to do it, you love it, you delight in it—there is no burden in it.

God acts out of love and not burden. This is the love of God.

TWO NATURES OR ONE?

I've often wondered why "hypocrite" was the insult of choice to hurl at those who believe in God. It's not as if the one slinging the accusation thinks they are morally superior—they will probably admit as fast as anyone that they aren't perfect. I guess it's just that they think Christians claim they are perfect, so spewing out the title 'hypocrite" appears to get them where they live. The word hypocrite means to put on another face—to be two faced—not a compliment in most cultures.

Integrity, on the other hand, is the opposite of hypocrisy. Living with integrity is living an "integrated" life. When you go to work, you are the same person you are at home, at a party, or church. Who you are on the outside is a reflection of who you are on the inside. You don't lose your integrity by doing something wrong, you lose it by being someone different. Integrity is more about being than about doing.

All of us, those of the faith and those outside the faith, have a big problem with people who act one way in front of one group and differently in front of another. But we have to admit we all struggle with it, even just a little.

The Apostle Peter suffered from some hypocrisy—even when he was the head of the newly forming church. And the Apostle Paul called him out on it.

"When Peter came to Antioch, I opposed him to his face, because he was clearly in the wrong. Before certain men came from James, he used to eat with the Gentiles. But when they arrived, he began to draw back and separate himself from the Gentiles because he was afraid of those who belonged to the circumcision group. The other Jews joined him in his hypocrisy, so that by their hypocrisy even Barnabas was led astray." (Galatians 2:11-13)

Way to go, Paul. Keep these guys accountable. Two-faced people are not Godly, and when you love God but serve money, you are a hypocrite.

"No one can serve two masters. Either he will hate the one and love the other, or he will be devoted to the one and despise the other. You cannot serve both God and money." (Matthew 6:24)

One of the ultimate hypocritical acts is to say you love God and want to serve Him, when you actually love money and do whatever you can to get it. No wonder it makes national news when a pastor or priest are caught skimming money from the church.

GOD AND MONEY

I wouldn't say I love money, but I do like it a lot, and if you're honest, you would have to admit it too. Pastors and Priests like money. They put in their time for the same stuff. Think of all the good things you can do with money—pay your rent or mortgage, feed your family, support your church or favorite charity, buy a car, and so on. Saying something is wrong with money itself makes no sense, it's like saying something is wrong with a pencil or a loaf of bread. It's just a thing.

But how can you serve money? Liking money is one thing,

but serving it is a confusing concept, so let me explain.

The other day I was outside mowing my lawn when my wife called to me, "Steve, the dog just did it on the carpet again. Are we going to replace this old carpet sometime soon?" Then the air conditioner broke and I had to organize the repairs. Then my tax bill came, and my mortgage notice, then my insurance bill—and I began to wonder, "Do I own this house or does it own me?"

When you spend most of your time thinking and working on your house, or when you spend most of your time planning and paying for your hobbies, car, or food, you may find these things may own you and not the other way around.

And when something owns you, you have become its slave. And what does a slave do? He serves his master. The problem isn't with money, it's a master and slave thing.

Who is your master—the things of God or the other things money can buy? Jesus says you can't serve them both, you have to chose.

When we love God and desire to please and honor him, this doesn't exclude us from thinking about money. Our years of trading education and experience for money are not hypocritical, self-serving acts. In today's world, we can't really live without money as a form of exchange, and a faithful person can't just drop off the grid in order to serve God.

Jesus is talking about our desires here, not whether or not we work for money. Our first priority is to please and honor God, and everything follows after that. If your first desire is to please and honor your ungodly boss in order to make lots of money, by definition you are not serving God. But if you love God and live to please and honor him, you can still make a living—even a very good living. Serving God and working for money are not mutually exclusive concepts.

"For even when we were with you, we gave you this rule: 'If a man will not work, he shall not eat.' We hear that some among you are idle. They are not busy; they are busybodies."

(2 Thessalonians 3:10-11)

"If anyone does not provide for his relatives, and especially for his immediate family, he has denied the faith ..." (1 Timothy 5:8)

Business at its nature is simply trade—exchanging what we have for what someone else has. We make it something good or evil the nature of by our desires, but at its nature trade is a benign activity.

Godliness at its nature is simply being like God and doing what he asks with a loving heart, desiring kindness, justice, righteousness, and giving grace.

If we serve money and try to serve God we will eventually be exposed for who we really are—hypocrites. But we can live in integrity when our focus is on loving, serving, and honoring God in our work. Our efforts to make money are part of our love for God and provide for the world.

"Do not love the world or anything in the world. If anyone loves the world, the love of the Father is not in him." (1 John 2:15)

If our deepest desires and longings are not to please and honor God, in very real and practical ways we show our true nature, and should question whether God's love is really part of us?

PRACTICAL THEOLOGY

One of the many things I love about scripture is how it portrays people. It tells the truth—shows people who they are, warts and all. David was a man after God's own heart, yet he slept with another man's wife and tried to cover it up by having him killed. Paul was at first one of the worst persecutors of the early followers of Jesus, but he became one of his most ardent disciples, telling us of his own failures. Abraham had an illegitimate son, and Peter denied he was a follower of Christ when the heat was on (actually all the apostles ran away for that matter.)

All these great men of faith were real people who earnestly desired to please and honor God. They failed sometimes, but they were accountable and turned back to their faithful lives. Scripture isn't just a lot of high lofty spiritual ideas. Most of it is practical wisdom for living. Performing our work in Godliness is a very practical affair.

"Have nothing to do with godless myths and old wives' tales; rather, train yourself to be Godly. For physical training is of some value, but godliness has value for all things, holding promise for both the present life and the life to come. This is a trustworthy saying that deserves full acceptance." (1 Timothy 4:7-9)

Paul tells us Godliness is not just a pursuit of heaven. There are very practical uses for Godliness in our lives at work, and this "deserves full acceptance." In other words, don't let anyone tell you otherwise.

Paul continues with some more practical theology.

"People who want to get rich fall into temptation and a trap and into many foolish and harmful desires that plunge men into ruin and destruction. For the love of money is a root of all kinds of evil. Some people, eager for money, have wandered from the faith and pierced themselves with many griefs. But you, man of God, flee from all this, and pursue righteousness, godliness, faith, love, endurance and gentleness. Fight the good fight of the faith. Take hold of the eternal life to which you were called when you made your good confession in the presence of many witnesses. (1 Timothy 6:10-12)

Business and Godliness are not rivals when you break them down to their core—their natures. They aren't incongruent when put in proper perspective—God first, everything else next. We are not trying to serve both God and money when we pursue a life of business. We are serving God by making money for Godly uses.

We aren't just framing walls, writing computer code, or teaching middle school students. We are building hospitals, making tools to connect the world and make it more productive, and influencing the next generation. And for what? Just to keep us busy? No. We are working because we have been commissioned from the highest level to perform the highest work—taking care of the physical and spiritual needs of the entire creation.

Why don't we get up every morning and say, "I get to do what God created me for today!"

Part Two

PRACTICALITY

Among the Trees and Watching for Wolves

7

Shrewd & Innocent
The Important Details

"Christianity needs a theology of work—and quickly. Unfortunately, though, constructing theology is a process that, like the great cathedrals of Europe, happens not over months and years, but over generations." Seward Hiltner, professor Princeton Theological Seminary

"How many graduate students does it take to screw in a light bulb? Only one, but it may take upwards of five years for him to get it done." Anonymous (surely a full-time student)

"Pray as though everything depended on God. Work as though everything depended on you." St. Augustine, Theologian, Bishop of Hippo, 4th century

BIG PICTURE – LITTLE PICTURE

Pondering the big picture while hovering at 30,000 feet isn't that exciting for the practical people who prefer to get straight to work. But to the artists and other lovers of philosophy, even the elementary-school version of philosophy used in this book, taking just one step without understanding the big picture is a chilling leap of blind faith.

So far we've discussed the world of work and Godliness with the big picture in mind—looking at the forest from 30,000 feet in the air. From way up there you can see the meadows, rivers, and rocks—the areas to avoid and the place you want to land. But now we're putting on our parachutes and jumping out of the plane. And when you land and find yourself in the middle of the dense trees, knowing wolves are lurking about, all you may have in mind is survival, not why the forest wolves exist. So watch out, as you plummet downward, the trees come at you pretty fast, and after you land and find yourself surrounded by wolves, you may be glad you spent time studying the forest from up high and getting your bearings.

INTEGRITY

"To the faithful you show yourself faithful, to the blameless you show yourself blameless, to the pure you show yourself pure, but to the crooked you show yourself shrewd." (Psalms 18:25-26)

David, in this, one of his many psalms, writes about how God shows himself to the different people of the world, and strangely he uses the same term Jesus does when sending out his disciples: shrewd. But, I have to admit, when first reading this verse it raised some doubts in my mind about God's character. Isn't this rather two-faced of God, acting one way to one group and another to another? I thought God, if anyone, was supposed to be consistent with everyone, no matter who they were.

From my years of study, one of the hallmarks of God's character is his consistency. Through history and throughout scripture we see him acting with the same righteousness, justice, kindness, and grace, so it goes against our view of fairness that God would not treat everyone the same. But being fair doesn't necessarily mean treating everyone the same, it should mean treating everyone by their needs. I may need glasses, but that doesn't mean everyone should get a pair just to be fair. It isn't unfair to treat people differently nor is it contrary to God's character to respond differently to different people in different situations.

The man who shakes his fist at God should be treated differently than a man who kneels in humility and prays. God loves them both, desires the best for them both, wants the same thing for them both, but they are in different places in life and need different things to get where God wants them to be. One man may need to be humbled to understand his relationship to others, and the humble man may need to be exalted to understand that by being made a special person with a special calling, there is a Godly pride. To one is given tough love, to another compassionate love—but fatherly love to both.

To be consistent in character is to be integrated in character—to have integrity. A man or woman of integrity, like God himself, carries the same character traits at all times and in all places, no matter who he or she is addressing, or whether they are in full public view, or all alone. You act out of who you are.

Responding to one person one way and a different person another doesn't mean you are inconsistent or lacking integrity. Like a loving father who wants the best for his children, we should act like him with the same motive—love. My thirsty neighbor needs a drink and my naked neighbor needs clothes so I shouldn't throw clothes at the thirsty and shower the naked with water. The constant is God's love—constant love, different actions.

BEING SHREWD

There is a common thread in the two statements of David and Jesus. David says God shows himself as shrewd, and Jesus urges his disciples to be shrewd and innocent. The thread is the people they are addressing—not the pure and Godly but the crooked and wicked.

"I am sending you out like sheep among wolves..." "But to the crooked you show yourself shrewd."

Just as we would respond differently to an attacking wolf than a grazing sheep, we should respond to the crooked differently than those who love God.

Suppose you were in the business of commercial real estate. Put yourself in the mind of a real estate broker who sees a piece of property with great potential. Suppose you approach the owner of the property and find him to be a kind and pleasant man. You enter his office and as you look around you find plaques of appreciation mounted on the walls, a picture of his smiling family on a missionary trip, and a Bible on his desk. After further investigation you find he is a leader in his church and a person of integrity.

As you begin discussing your ideas for developing the property, you might consider partnering with the owner. He brings the land to the deal, and you have the vision and experience to get the idea to the market for its highest and best use, so why not go into the deal as partners?

But what if you approach the owner and find him to be a foul man—insulting people you know to be honest, telling stories of his selfish exploits, and as you enter his office you see a photo of his family on the wall, but from a drunken party, and you find pornography on his desk. There is no way a godly man would want to become partners with a man like this. So instead, you just ask him what price he would accept for his land, buy it, and go on your way. You can avoid partnering with him and continue with your business. You can remain kind, just, and righteous in all your dealings, but you respond to him differently than the other guy.

Having been in the real estate world for many years, I believe a crooked person may actually have respect for a Godly person who acts shrewdly. The crooked person's stereotypical view of a Godly businessman may be a weak naïve person who he can take advantage of (like a wolf). But when we act shrewdly (cunning and crafty), you gain a measure of respect with him, which may gain a measure of respect for the God whom you represent.

But being shrewd is more than just being wise. There is a craftiness, a creativity to it.

PAUL AND KING DAVID

When Paul was on his missionary journey, it took him to Greece, the intellectual capital of the world. But look how Paul dealt with these intellectuals.

"While Paul was waiting for them in Athens, he was greatly distressed to see that the city was full of idols. So he reasoned in the synagogue with the Jews and the God-fearing Greeks, as well as in the marketplace day by day with those who happened to be there.

"A group of Epicurean and Stoic philosophers began to dispute with him. Some of them asked, 'What is this babbler trying to say?' Others remarked, 'He seems to be advocating foreign gods.' They said this because Paul was preaching the good news about Jesus and the resurrection. Then they took him and brought him to a meeting of the Areopagus, where they said to him, 'May we know what this new teaching is that you are presenting? You are bringing some strange ideas to our ears, and we want to know what they mean.' (All the Athenians and the foreigners who lived there spent their time doing nothing but talking about and listening to the latest ideas.) Paul then stood up in the meeting of the Areopagus and said: 'Men of Athens! I see that in every way you are very religious. For as I walked around and looked carefully at your objects of worship, I even found an altar with this inscription: to an unknown god. Now what you worship as something unknown I am going to proclaim to you.

"The God who made the world and everything in it is the Lord of heaven and earth and does not live in temples built by hands... 'For in him we live and move and have our being.' As some of your own poets have said, 'We are his offspring.'

Therefore since we are God's offspring, we should not think that the divine being is like gold or silver or stone—an image made by man's design and skill. In the past God overlooked such ignorance, but now he commands all people everywhere to repent. For he has set a day when he will judge the world with justice by the man he has appointed. He has given proof of this to all men by raising him from the dead." When they heard about the resurrection of the dead, some of them sneered, but others said, We want to hear you again on this subject. At that, Paul left the Council. A few men became followers of Paul and believed." (Acts 17: 16-34)

Paul was wise but he was also shrewd—there is a slight but important difference.

To be wise, you need to know the truth about three things. First, you must know the truth, the actual cold hard reality, about yourself. You should know your strengths and weaknesses, your bents, where you shine and where you may fail. David, before he became king, was a short, stocky kid, but he knew he was great with a sling. He had taken some smooth stones and killed lions and bears with it in the past. So when he faced the eight foot tall Goliath, the best warrior of the enemy of Israel, what do you think he turned to? His sling. (And just in case he missed the first time, or Goliath's four relatives were nearby, he picked up four extra stones.)

Before you walk into any battle, know whether it is best to retreat or charge. Paul was trained by one of the best scholars in Jerusalem, Gamaliel the leader of the Sanhedrin, so he was ready for the Greek philosophers. In stark contract, I experienced the mental beating of a lifetime when as a young, inexperienced university student, I tried to argue the benefits of God and Godliness with someone trained in the history and art of philosophy. The truth, the cold hard reality, was that I wasn't ready. It was bloody.

Second, you should know the truth, the actual cold hard reality, about your opponent, your friend, or with whomever your are dealing.

Paul knew the Epicurean and Stoic philosophies and apparently knew the temperament of the men he faced. They were deep thinkers, but they also liked to hear themselves talk and were lovers of the latest philosophical fashions.

David new his opponent was an experienced and enormous warrior and stayed a distance away from Goliath to sling his stones. A close battle would have been his end.

And third, you should know the truth, the actual cold hard reality about your circumstances. You could be the best trained warrior on the battlefield opposing someone you know you can beat, but if there are a thousand warriors directly behind your opponent, circumstances may dictate a call for reinforcements.

Paul had spent days working with the crowds and his opponents. Since the Areopagus was such a popular place, I would guess Paul had watched debates there before. I doubt David would have gone all the way into the Philistine's camp to fight Goliath (even though he appeared to have faith enough to do it).

Knowing the truth about your strengths and weaknesses and those of your opponent, and knowing the circumstances you find yourself in are definitely wise. But to be shrewd is to add creativity to your wisdom—a cunning, craftiness like Paul does with the Greeks. Paul doesn't just begin preaching as he would in a synagogue, he begins with a reference to their rich culture of philosophy and poetry to gain their interest, then point them to the truth.

WISE AND SHREWD

Sometimes, however, depending on your audience, shrewdness requires subtly and craftiness. Take Solomon the young king who prayed for wisdom instead of riches. After God answered his prayer, he gave him a chance to be shrewd.

"Now two prostitutes came to the king and stood before him. One of them said, 'My lord, this woman and I live in the same house. I had a baby while she was there with me. The third day after my child was born, this woman also had a baby. We were alone; there was no one in the house but the two of us. During the night this woman's son died because she lay on him. So she got up in the middle of the night and took my son from my side while I your servant was asleep. She put him by her breast and put her dead son by my breast. The next morning, I got up to nurse my son—and he was dead! But when I looked at him closely in the morning light, I saw that it wasn't the son I had borne.' The other woman said, 'No! The living one is my son; the dead one is yours.' But the first one insisted, 'No! The dead one is yours; the living one is mine.' And so they argued before the king. The king said, 'This one says, 'My son is alive and your son is dead,' while that one says, 'No! Your son is dead and mine is alive.'"

"Then the king said, 'Bring me a sword.' So they brought a sword for the king. He then gave an order: 'Cut the living child in two and give half to one and half to the other.' The woman whose son was alive was filled with compassion for her son and said to the king, 'Please, my lord, give her the living baby! Don't kill him!' But the other said, 'Neither I nor you shall have him. Cut him in two!' Then the king gave his ruling: 'Give the living baby to the first woman. Do not kill him; she is his mother.' When all Israel heard the verdict the king had given, they held the king in awe, because they saw that he had wisdom from God to administer justice." (1 Kings 3:16—28)

Now that's shrewd.

I don't think Solomon just got tired of their arguing, decided to end the dispute with killing the baby and then accidentally discovered the real mother. I believe he acted with the wisdom of God (or from God) to discover the true mother and solidify his role as a wise king of Israel. He had a creative idea to find justice, didn't reveal it until it was appropriate, and then acted on it—and the truth came out. By acting shrewdly, all the wicked people who saw him in action, the other lying mothers (or business people), took warning that they were dealing with an extraordinarily Godly man. They had a whole new respect for him and the God he served.

There is a creativity to shrewdness that goes beyond wisdom.

Jesus was shrewd when dealing with the religious leaders who tried to trap him with flattery.

"Then the Pharisees went out and laid plans to trap him in his words. They sent their disciples to him along with the Herodians. 'Teacher,' they said, 'we know you are a man of integrity and that you teach the way of God in accordance with the truth. You aren't swayed by men, because you pay no attention to who they are. Tell us then, what is your opinion? Is it right to pay taxes to Caesar or not?' But Jesus, knowing their evil intent, said, 'You hypocrites, why are you trying to trap me? Show me the coin used for paying the tax.' They brought him a denarius, and he asked them, 'Whose portrait is this? And whose inscription?' 'Caesar's,' they replied. Then he said to them, 'Give to Caesar what is Caesar's, and to God what is God's.' When they heard this, they were amazed. So they left him and went away." (Matthew 22:15-22)

I don't think Jesus had any special insight into their motives. I believe he knew who his opponents were and responded accordingly, like we can when we are shrewd.

"Hearing that Jesus had silenced the Sadducees, the Pharisees got together. One of them, an expert in the law, tested him with this question: 'Teacher, which is the greatest commandment in the Law?' Jesus replied: 'Love the Lord your God with all your heart and with all your soul and with all your mind.' This is the first and greatest commandment. And the second is like it: 'Love your neighbor as yourself.' All the Law and the Prophets hang on these two commandments."

"While the Pharisees were gathered together, Jesus asked

them, 'What do you think about the Christ? Whose son is he?' 'The son of David,' they replied. He said to them, 'How is it then that David, speaking by the Spirit, calls him 'Lord?'' For he says, 'The Lord said to my Lord: 'Sit at my right hand until I put your enemies under your feet.' 'If then David calls him 'Lord,' how can he be his son?' No one could say a word in reply, and from that day on no one dared to ask him any more questions. (Matthew 22:41-46)

Sometimes we are on defense, fending off the wolves. Other times we are to go on offense and confront our opponent head on, but with respect—all the time as a representative of the God who is kind, just, and righteous.

THE BOTTOM LINE

"Wisdom will save you from the ways of wicked men, from men whose words are perverse." (Proverbs 2:12)

"How much better to get wisdom than gold, to choose understanding rather than silver." (Proverbs 16:16)

"Buy the truth and do not sell it; get wisdom, discipline and understanding." (Proverbs 23:23)

"He who trusts in himself is a fool, who walks in wisdom is kept safe." (Proverbs 28:26)

Scripture is full of examples of shrewd and innocent action. I could tell of Daniel as an exiled young man remaining true to his vows to God, shrewdly approached the man who held his life in his hands. There is Joseph devising a business plan for his boss, Pharaoh, and saving the lives of his people and increasing the authority of his boss. And there are others, all acting with the wisdom of mature men of God but with shrewd creativity and innocent hearts.

We can learn from the their examples—even in our time and within the business world of sales, marketing, manufacturing, and professional services. We work in a world of greed, competition, and risk supported by an economic system unheard of in biblical times. But the lessons are the same—our hearts should be the same.

To the pure, be and act pure (with an innocent heart and selfless motives), but to the crooked and wicked, be and act shrewdly (creative, crafty and wise). To both, be the blameless person you are before God. Each will respect you for it, and prayerfully they may see God in it.

Be Godly and you will act Godly. When you are something (Godly) you simply and naturally act that way.

God is more interested in who you are than what you do—because when you work on who you are, you can't help but act accordingly.

8
Wealth, Ownership and Choice

"Wherever true Christianity spreads, it must cause diligence and frugality which, in the natural course of things, must beget riches! And riches naturally beget pride, love of the world, and every temper that is destructive of Christianity. Now, if there be no way to prevent this, Christianity is inconsistent with itself and, of consequence, cannot stand, cannot continue long among any people since, wherever it generally prevails, it saps its own foundation." John Wesley, founder of the Methodist church, his Sermon 87 on the Danger of Riches

"By your wisdom and understanding you have gained wealth for yourself and amassed gold and silvery in your treasuries. By your great skill in trading you have increased your wealth, and because of your wealth your heart has grown proud." (Ezekiel 28:4) Ezekiel, 3rd major prophet of Israel and writer of the Book of Ezekiel.

"I can run. I can jump. I can block shots. I can dunk. But I can't take pride in that. I'm successful because God gave me the ability." David Robinson, NBA Hall of Fame, philanthropist, founder David Robinson Foundation

"There are two kinds of people: those who say to God, 'Thy will be done,' and those to whom God says, 'All right, then, have it your way.'" C.S. Lewis, The Screwtape Letters, 1943

"The plans of the diligent lead to profit as surely as haste leads to poverty" (Proverbs 21:5) Solomon, King of Israel in 10th century B.C., philosopher, multiple billionaire in today's dollars based on gold holdings alone.

WORK AND WEALTH

Someone tell me why wealth has become so unpopular? Nowadays no one dares speak of receiving a high paying job—even if it's for very specialized work performed exceptionally well. As I talk to people moving from school into the business world they describe their work in more altruistic, non-business terms: "I'm an architect, but I plan on going to the Sudan to dig water wells for the villagers." Or, "I'm a banker, but I want to work for a nonprofit that places workers and money into undeveloped areas of the world."

This is all well and good, but what ever happened to working for good-old profit?

Please don't misunderstand me. These goals for the Sudan and nonprofits are noble and Godly things for sure, but there is a subtle implication in their statements—"for" profit companies are not as noble or pure as nonprofits. Nonprofits are somehow cleaner, less stained by the money grubbing world. I'm glad working people don't want to be tainted by the world, but their premise is a false one.

Let me tell you a little biblical secret. It's OK to be wealthy. It's OK to be just a little wealthier than your neighbor. It's OK to be vastly wealthy accruing billions upon billions of dollars, owning stock, or owning corporations. In fact, God has great use for the wealthy—and the poor.

It's even ok to pray for wealth. Ask Jabez. "Jabez was more honorable than his brothers... Jabez cried out to the God of Israel, 'Oh, that you would bless me and enlarge my territory! Let your hand be with me, and keep me from harm so that I will be free from pain.' And God granted his request." (1 Chronicles 4:1-10)

I wonder if God new something about Jabez, that he was responsible and answered his request with "Yes." At the same time, I wonder if there is something within me that would cause God to answer "No way!"

GOD AND WEALTH

God knows some who desire wealth, and he says yes. Some inherit wealth and lose it, while others inherit wealth and use it well. Others don't ask for it, and God gives them wealth beyond their wildest dreams. Take Solomon, the son of King David.

"That night God appeared to Solomon and said to him, 'Ask for whatever you want me to give you.' Solomon answered God, 'You have shown great kindness to David my father and have made me king in his place. Now, Lord God, let your promise to my father David be confirmed, for you have made me king over a people who are as numerous as the dust of the earth. Give me wisdom and knowledge, that I may lead this people, for who is able to govern this great people of yours?"

"God said to Solomon, 'Since this is your heart's desire and you have not asked for wealth, riches or honor, nor for the death of your enemies, and since you have not asked for a long life but for wisdom and knowledge to govern my people over whom I have made you king, therefore wisdom and knowledge will be given you. And I will also give you wealth, riches and honor, such as no king who was before you ever had and none after you will have." (2 Chronicles 1:7-12)

No wonder Solomon became the wealthiest and most honored king of his time. Some estimate his gold reserves alone, not including other property or businesses, was worth billions, if not trillions, in today's dollars. God can bless when he really wants to.

Wealth and profit are not evil things, as Solomon says, "When God gives any man wealth and possessions, and enables him to enjoy them, to accept his lot and be happy in his work—this is a gift of God." (Ecclesiastes 5:19)

Abraham was a wealthy man when God called him to move his family and find the land of promise. Why didn't God tell him to leave all he had and follow him? Possibly because Abraham's wealth was not in the way of his heart. He trusted God, and God used him and his wealth. Job was no pauper either. Even though he lost it all, it was all given back at the end of this life. Joseph became one of the wealthiest and most powerful men in Egypt. God has no problem with wealth.

So there you have it. It is OK to be wealthy. God has his hand in it.

WEALTH, DECEIT AND FALSE IDENTITY

But with wealth comes responsibility and the potential for some large problems. In Jesus words, "From everyone who has been given much, much will be demanded; and from the one who has been entrusted with much, much more will be asked." (Luke 12:48)

Jesus tells a parable about a farmer (a sewer) throwing his seed on his field, and in it he describes four types of soil—the hard soil of the dirt roads between fields, the soil full of rocks, the soil which grows thorns, and then the good, fertile soil. Jesus uses the soils as a metaphor for the heart. Some hearts are hard, others rocky, others are choked by wealth and the cares of the world and other are receptive and fertile. But to the issue of wealth, Jesus says:

"The one who received the seed that fell among the thorns is the man who hears the word, but the worries of this life and the deceitfulness of wealth choke it, making it unfruitful." (Matthew 13:22)

Wealth, in some strange way, can be deceitful. It lies to us, or because of it we lie to ourselves. Wealth can give us a false sense of identity and it can give us a false sense of security. And to many who have wealth, it is a burden.

I've been around the world of athletics for a good part of my life. During that time I've had chances to see some of the most gifted athletes in the world—and I say gifted for a very specific reason. There is absolutely no way these athletes have worked to get what they have. Yes, some do work hard and get better, but I'm talking about the gift of raw talent, of height and weight, combined with synaptic firing speed. These guys are fabulously wealthy with athletic talent.

Although I was gifted athletically, I could never say I had anything to do with it. God must have played with my genetic make up—a little great grandfather here, some extra good nutrition there, a special touch of God, and tah-dah, there I was—a large, fast athlete.

I knew who I was—a normal guy blessed with a unique gift—and there are many others like me who looked at their gifts and were thankful and humbled by them. And if you took away our gift we would just be the same normal guy.

For other athletes however, those given a wealth of physique and ability, for some reason they look at their gift and are not thankful or humbled, but prideful. For whatever reason (poverty, abusive parenting, or just plain arrogance) they have the opposite reaction. They build their whole world around sports, and because they link their identity with their gift, if you take it away their world crumbles.

It's the same with those who receive other types of wealth. I know women whose worlds revolve around their beauty. There are scholars whose mental giftedness and lofty theories have earned them degrees and celebrity. All are vastly wealthy, and some are thankful but others arrogant.

Monetary wealth may not be an obvious gift. There are

many who work long, hard, wisely, and give up many things in their lives—some families and some integrity. But I find their responses are usually similar to athletes—they are either humbled or arrogant. Their very identities are wrapped up in their wealth, and when God takes it away, they crumble—falling to their knees embarrassed to finally realize they are merely normal people like the rest of us. God has all sorts of uses for wealth—sometimes humbling the prideful, and sometimes blessing the humble.

"A rich man may be wise in his own eyes, but a poor man who has discernment sees through him." (Proverbs 28:11)

WEALTH AND FALSE SECURITY

Wealth can deceive us by giving us a false sense of identity, but wealth can also deceive us by giving us a false sense of security. Jesus tells a story of a man whose security was wrapped up in his wealth.

"And he told them this parable: 'The ground of a certain rich man produced a good crop. He thought to himself, 'What shall I do? I have no place to store my crops.' Then he said, 'This is what I'll do. I will tear down my barns and build bigger ones, and there I will store all my grain and my goods. And I'll say to myself, 'You have plenty of good things laid up for many years. Take life easy; eat, drink and be merry.' But God said to him, 'You fool! This very night your life will be demanded from you. Then who will get what you have prepared for yourself?'

"This is how it will be with anyone who stores up things for himself but is not rich toward God." (Luke 12: 16-21)

Jesus later tells another story of a young man who probably inherited his wealth and had tried his best to live a good life. But he missed the point when it came to understanding where true wealth lies.

"A certain ruler asked him, 'Good teacher, what must I do

to inherit eternal life?' 'Why do you call me good?' Jesus answered. "No one is good—except God alone. You know the commandments: 'Do not commit adultery, do not murder, do not steal, do not give false testimony, honor your father and mother.'"

"All these I have kept since I was a boy," he said.

"When Jesus heard this, he said to him, 'You still lack one thing. Sell everything you have and give to the poor, and you will have treasure in heaven. Then come, follow me.

"When he heard this, he became very sad, because he was a man of great wealth.

"Jesus looked at him and said, 'How hard it is for the rich to enter the kingdom of God! ...' Those who heard this asked, 'Who then can be saved?' Jesus replied, 'What is impossible with men is possible with God.' Peter said to him, 'We have left all we had to follow you!' 'I tell you the truth,' Jesus said to them, 'no one who has left home or wife or brothers or parents or children for the sake of the kingdom of God will fail to receive many times as much in this age and, in the age to come, eternal life." (Luke 18:18-30)

Is there anything wrong with being wealthy? We've already answered that question—no. But Jesus does strongly suggest that wealth can be a big hindrance to spiritual maturity.

The problem with these two guys was not wealth, it was that they believed their security was in their wealth. They trusted it more than they trusted God.

WEALTH, BURDEN, AND RELATIVITY

I know it may be hard to believe, but wealth can actually be a burden as well.

"Whoever loves money never has money enough; whoever loves wealth is never satisfied with his income. This, too, is meaningless. As goods increase, so do those who consume them. And what benefit are they to the owner except to feast his eyes on them? The sleep of a laborer is sweet, whether he eats little or much, but the abundance of a rich man permits him no sleep." (Ecclesiastes 5: 10-12)

As your wealth increases, so does your entourage. Sometimes as your wealth increases, so does your family's appetite for things—houses, cars, boats, clothes, trips, etc. What good is your wealth than just to watch it as it sifts like sand through your fingers.

I grew up in a family of artists. We never starved, but I recall when money was tight and we ate a lot of beans (which are not so bad when your mother knows how to cook). But we had a roof over our head, and my parents never suggested that our world was coming to an end (because it wasn't). We lived in a small town with other families of similar socioeconomic conditions. We felt normal.

My wife on the other hand grew up in a different world. Her normal was different than mine. She was the daughter of a medical doctor with a country club membership, mother in a bridge club—the upper middle class world. Compared to my family they lived pretty well. However her family grew up around a wealthy oil-rich crowd from Texas, so comparatively they didn't feel wealthy at all. They just had one house, not a mountain retreat or second home on the beach. They went on vacation just once a year and didn't "summer in Europe." Her normal was different from their normal, which was different from my normal.

Wealth is a very subjective and relative thing.

I recall a young man returning from a mission trip to South America, telling us of the poverty of the region and the happiness of the children living there, said, "They don't even know how poor they are."

OWNERSHIP AND CHOICE

When describing wealth, we typically speak of posses-

112

sions—a wealth of things (money, homes, cars), or we think about possessing a wealth of abilities or characteristics (athleticism, beauty, or brains). It's about possessions.

But I have a question. What do we actually posses anyway? What does it mean to actually own something?

Take your home for example. When you buy a home with a mortgage on it, you have the right to use the home, but you can't say you actually own it. The bank owns it until you pay it off. If you destroy your home, you would still have to pay the monthly payment—you just wouldn't be able to live in it. And if you stop paying, who comes and gets your home? The rightful owner—the bank.

What about something you've paid for—say your car? If you have your car paid for, you would think you have use of it all the time. But if you're convicted of drunk driving or have too many speeding tickets, you may forfeit your rights to drive the car. What use is a car you can't drive? You own it, but not if you can't really use it.

Let's take this notion of ownership to the extreme. Do you own your own body? You would think so. But there are thousands of young men and women who join the armed forces and are thrown into combat without their approval, and are killed. Who owns your body? It could be the Army, or your family if you're lying on your deathbed, or your jailer if you lived in Iran or North Korea and suspected of a crime.

Let's take it comically one step further. If an evil army came from outer space and conquered the USA, enslaving all its citizens, would you have the right to own or use your cell phone anymore? Probably not. When evil aliens conquer earth, your home, your car, everything you own would be forfeited because the civil authorities you have come to trust to protect those "rights" of ownership, have gone away.

Ownership is not just possession. It has more to do with authority than the privileges of use.

DR. VIKTOR FRANKL

Dr. Viktor Frankl was a prominent Austrian psychiatrist and one of the thousands of Jews thrown into concentration camps when the Nazis came to power. In his book *Man's Search for Meaning*, Dr. Frankl describes his life in the concentration camps, his separation from and the ultimate death of his wife and parents, and the despair facing everyone around him every day. If you want to understand ownership, enter the world of a concentration camp with Dr. Frankl.

Although faced with brutal horrors, many prisoners found a way to live through it. Dr. Frankl writes, "If a prisoner felt that he could no longer endure the realities of camp life, he found a way out in his mental life—an invaluable opportunity to dwell in the spiritual domain, the one that the SS was unable to destroy. Spiritual life strengthened the prisoner, helped him adapt, and thereby improved his chances of survival."

One of Dr. Frankl's observations relate to the one thing we actually own—our choices. "The experiences of camp life show that man does have a choice of action. There were enough examples, often of a heroic nature, which proved that apathy could be overcome, irritability suppressed. Man can preserve a vestige of spiritual freedom, of independence of mind, even in such terrible conditions of psychic and physical stress.

"We who lived in concentration camps can remember the men who walked through the huts comforting others, giving away their last piece of bread. They may have been few in number, but they offer sufficient proof that everything can be taken from a man but one thing: the last of the human freedoms—to choose one's attitude in any given set of circumstances, to choose one's own way."

The reality and cruelty of a concentration camp proves that ultimately we own nothing - there is no possession an authority can't take from us—except for our choices. We are in control of our choices. Like the heroic man who gave away is last piece of bread and by doing so chose to die, ultimately we have this one possession, our will, our choice.

STEWARDSHIP VS OWNERSHIP

These examples help me understand what God means when he says we are stewards of what we posses, not actual owners. Ownership is granted by someone who has authority over it—a prison guard, or a government who protects those rights of property. We are granted authority to own our homes, our cars, and our cell phones by the laws and protection of the entity who can grant that authority. We are granted a license to drive from our local state, who receives authority from the federal government—currently the supreme authority when it comes to these kinds of rights.

This is not necessarily a bad or good thing. It's just the way it is and always has been. Originally the family unit had authority over your rights. Then kings were granted authority, then emperor kings who held religious power as well, and now citizens of our democracies.

But those who love God and live to please and honor him understand who is in control and who has real authority—the one who actually owns it all. These guys understand they just posses things on loan from the one with authority, so they see themselves as stewards of their wealth and not owners—servants given temporary charge of property. There is a small but very important difference as illustrated by Jesus in the Parable of the Talents.

There once was "a man going on a trip. He called together his servants and gave them money to invest for him while he was gone. He gave five bags of gold to one, two bags of gold to another, and one bag of gold to the last—dividing it in proportion to their abilities—and then left on his trip.

"The servant who received the five bags of gold began immediately to invest the money and soon doubled it. The servant with two bags of gold also went right to work and doubled the money...

"After a long time their master returned from his trip and called them to give an account of how they had used his money. The servant to whom he had entrusted the five bags of gold said, 'Sir, you gave me five bags of gold to invest, and I have doubled the amount.' The master was full of praise. 'Well done, my good and faithful servant. You have been faithful in handling this small amount, so now I will give you many more responsibilities. Let's celebrate together!' (Matthew 25:14-21)

A good steward acts like the owner, but knows he's not the true owner. A steward is granted authority to use those things provided him by the real owner. He buys and sells. He negotiates prices and competes in the marketplace. He takes on risks and employees to be productive—just like any owner does. He acts just like the owner, but there is a difference. The difference is the heart of the steward, his motives.

When I am the owner, my possessions are under my care and control. When I buy and sell, negotiate and compete, I am accountable only to me. I have the authority to risk it all and possibly even destroy my livelihood, so I may hold onto them tightly (my identity and security may be wrapped in my possessions). But when I am finished with my work, I did it all for me. I can look forward to using the profit for whatever I chose.

But when I am a steward, my responsibilities are different. The possessions given me are still under my care and control, just as in the parable, I immediately start doing what my master asks me to do, buy and sell, negotiate and compete in the marketplace. But the important difference is that since I don't actually own the things and my livelihood and future are not at risk (since they are in the hands of the master), I am free to hold the possessions more loosely—and may even take more risks. I do what I do, not for me, but looking forward to what my master thinks of my work. And when I am finished, I look forward to giving it all back to the rightful owner—my master.

CHOICE

"The earth is the Lord's, and everything in it." (Psalm 24:1)

God owns everything. He made it all and he can take it all if he wants. We are just granted the right to use our possessions from the one with ultimate authority. And he gives them to whomever he pleases. It sure looks like we own our possessions, and we sure act like we do, but we're just living in the reality and safety of God's authority and enjoying our use of his possessions.

The only real possessions we have, the only things we have true authority over are our choices. I wonder if that's why scripture tells us we will be judged by our choices. It's the only thing we actually own and are responsible for. It's the only thing that God gave us full rights to—our own little piece of sovereignty. No one can take these from us. Thank God we have a judge that is kind, just, and righteous, who knows our heart and motives and knows why we make our choices.

"For the word of God is living and active. Sharper than any double-edged sword, it penetrates even to dividing soul and spirit, joints and marrow; it judges the thoughts and attitudes of the heart." (Hebrews 4:12)

"Therefore judge nothing before the appointed time; wait till the Lord comes. He will bring to light what is hidden in darkness and will expose the motives of men's hearts. At that time each will receive his praise from God." (1 Corinthians 4:5)

PROFIT AND WEALTH

Living and working with a heart to please and honor God, in godliness, often times provides strange results—profit and wealth.

"For bodily discipline is only of little profit, but godliness is profitable for all things, since it holds promise for the present life and also for the life to come." (1 Timothy 4:8 – NASB)

Yes, it says Godliness is profitable in the present life. But even so, let's not put the cart before the horse. The purpose of business is not, or shouldn't be, profit and wealth. Focusing on money and profit perverts the reason for working. Focusing on money and profit usually fosters short term vision and decisions—corners to be cut and shortcuts to be taken with the aim of making more money instead of working more efficiently and making your service or product more beneficial.

Fulfilling your calling for work and working as if God were your boss fosters productivity greater than most companies can imagine. The Puritans, one of the first American communities were committed to the idea of doing everything for God with the highest quality and integrity, and they eventually became very prosperous. That same commitment held the seeds of it's own downfall—the more creative and productive you become, the more wealth you generate, and wealth has the potential of deceiving everyone into a false sense of identity and security.

Becoming wealthy isn't that hard. The key to monetary wealth is simple—spend less than you make over a long period of time. Of course many gain wealth because of great ideas culminating in IPOs (Initial Public Offerings) or inheriting from their relatives or becoming personal injury lawyers, but they are the exceptions. Most wealth comes from frugality and integrity.

In their book *The Millionaire Next Door*, Thomas J. Stanley and William D. Danko revealed that eighty percent of America's millionaires are first generation rich, contrary to those who have you believe that wealth is usually inherited. Twenty percent of millionaires are retired and fifty percent own a business.

THERE IS NO SPENDING – ONLY INVESTING

We need to choose a different paradigm—a shift in thinking about work, wealth, Godliness and the use of money. Our current paradigm (our perception without thinking about it) revolves around spending, "We spend our time to make money in order to spend it on something else." It's all about spending.

In reality we are not spending time making money and we are not spending the money. We are investing. We are investing our time and talents for a return on that investment (money), and we are investing that money in something else (food, housing, or ministry). There is no such thing as spending, only investing. I know it may sound somewhat semantic, but it's important.

It's easy to understand investing in a stock or company—we exchange our money (buy stock) and expect a return on that investment. The money didn't go away by spending it, it was traded for something else of value—value traded for value.

Anytime we spend (or exchange) our money we are actually investing in whatever we purchase. We don't spend our money on stock, we invest. We don't spend our money on a house, we invest in our shelter. We don't spend our money on food, we invest in our bodies. We don't spend our money on recreational activities like golf, hunting or shopping, we are investing in rest and peace of mind. The question is: Are we making good investments.

"Do not be deceived, God is not mocked; for whatever a man sows, this he will also reap." (Galatians 6:7)

We are only investing (sowing) and we are always reaping the benefits from those investments. Investing in a candy bar and a movie can be very good investment in our relaxation, but investing too much money in candy bars or other comfort food will reap a fat belly and clogged arteries. We do reap what we sow.

To the one who loves God and lives to please and honor him, choices and paradigm shifts are a way of life. He would say, "I once thought it was all about me and mine, and now I know it's all about Him and others. I once thought it was about earning enough points to get into heaven, but now I realize I could never get there under my own strength. I once thought I deserved everything, and now I know I deserve nothing, but it is all a gift from God."

By choosing a new paradigm (specifically for this chapter, changing our view of the world of wealth) and by realizing wealth is a gift to be a steward of, we are on the road to seeing our work and wealth through different eyes.

Paul tells his young protégé, Timothy, "Tell those who are rich in this present world not to be arrogant nor to put their hope in wealth, which is so uncertain, but to put their hope in God, who richly provides us with everything for our enjoyment. Command them to do good, to be rich in good deeds, and to be generous and willing to share. In this way they will lay up treasure for themselves as a firm foundation for the coming age, so that they may take hold of the life that is truly life." (Timothy 6:17-19)

9

Greed, Self-interest and Desire

"The point is, ladies and gentleman, that greed—for lack of a better word—is good. Greed is right. Greed works. Greed clarifies, cuts through, and captures the essence of the evolutionary spirit. Greed, in all of its forms—greed for life, for money, for love, knowledge—has marked the upward surge of mankind." Gordon Gekko, from the movie Wall Street (Mr. Gekko's character was based on an investor named Ivan Boesky who gave such a speech to an enthusiastic audience at the University of California Berkeley in 1986 shortly before he was arrested)

"Greed is the genesis of all economic activity." Wikipedia (Though not a harbinger of exhaustive research, you can at least say that the internet encyclopedia Wikipedia's comment on greed reflects the views of many young business people.)

"Christianity proposes not to extinguish our natural desires. It promises to bring the desires under just control and direct them to their true object." William Wilberforce, member of Parliament, through his leadership abolished slavery in England

"Put to death, therefore, whatever belongs to your earthly nature: sexual immorality, impurity, lust, evil desires and greed, which is idolatry." (Colossians 3:5) Apostle Paul, to his friends at the church in Colossae

WHAT IS GREED?

When I think of greed I picture wealthy Wall Street fat cats smoking big cigars in their dark wooden-paneled rooms, sipping brandy and laughing aloud as they brag about their latest business exploits—exploiting their employees, exploiting their investors, exploiting everyone (Insert Gordon Gekko here).

But to get a little closer to home, I picture a plumber who was asked to fix a leaky faucet at our home, insisting to my wife it will cost $500 to replace the $100 part. He knows she's not mechanically inclined. He also looks over our house and the neighborhood, sizes up the situation, and demands twice the money he normally would. Why not? He may get it. Is this guy greedy?

Or there's the evil banker waiting for the elderly widow to stop making payments so he can foreclose on her house and sell it. What about the ticket scalper or the insurance salesman or the hedge fund manager? All these guys want to make lots of money. Are they greedy?

An economist would say, "There is no such thing as greed when you speak of commerce." Greed is a moral issue. Scientists and economists don't deal in morality, they just deal in facts (what is, not what ought to be). The workings of the economy is just a lot of buying and selling, the distribution and redistribution of resources, and if someone gathers up a lot of resources, they are just wealthy not greedy.

What does greed actually mean? Raw, unfettered Capitalism? Is it just self-interest taken to extreme? Or is greed in essence just our desire for things?

DESIRE ITSELF

We all desire something—some things more than others. In fact there are some desires that are overwhelming—food, shelter, companionship, love—and these desires could motivate us to do almost anything to fulfill them, good or bad. Some would say our very desires are the problem, and we should extinguish them all.

Os Guinness alludes to the problem of desire from the eastern religious perspective—that desire itself is the problem. "This view perceives desire not as a good thing that can go wrong but as essentially evil. Desires keep us bound to the world of suffering and illusion. The solution, therefore, is not to fulfill desire but to stop it, finally transcending it altogether in the state of 'extinguishedness' called nirvana. Though it appears sophisticated, consistent, and practical within its own circle of assumptions, this Eastern view is radically world-denying. As such its appeal to a culture as world-affirming as ours is inevitably limited."

Unlike many eastern views, the Judeo-Christian worldview is world-affirming—it accepts a real and physical world that is obvious and exists on its own and apart from ourselves. We believe there are such things as good desires—desiring to please and honor God, the desire to eat a healthy meal, or do good work for our family and others. So we don't conclude that all desires are evil or a form of greed. We were created and are the image bearers of a kind, just and righteous God, who created us as self-willed beings who have desires—some desires are bad but some desires are very good.

DESIRE FOR MORE

So if desire itself isn't the problem, maybe it's the strong desire for something more that makes us greedy? I have one dollar but I really want two. I have one pair of shoes, but I really desire five. It's about desiring more.

But am I greedy if I have a strong desire for a higher paying job? Am I greedy if I want a larger home to house my growing family? I don't think so.

Maybe it's wealth that makes you greedy. Consider those Wall Street fat cats. Some of them make hundreds of millions of dollars a year and all they do is sit in their big offices, buy stocks or commodities, and sell them for a profit. Buy low, sell high, make commission. These guys are basically high stakes risk takers, and some may be greedy but others may not. We should be careful with your judgments. These guys haven't done anything wrong when they makes millions, they just reaped the reward from their resources, ideas, or investments. There may actually be a fat cat or two who gives more money away than you make in a lifetime, and to a cause that's dear to your heart.

Don't we do exactly the same thing they do when we sell a house or discuss raising our salary with an employer? Are we being greedy by desiring the highest price we can get?

Many of us are too quick to judge the very wealthy. We look down on the stock brokers, the professional athletes, or the debutants with their inherited millions, while we don't give a second thought to the actor who makes $10 million a picture (each actor in the Friends television series earned $100 million over the span of the show). We don't mind when the person who invented the latest household convenience makes a vast amount of money. Remember the ShamWow, or the Snuggy? They sold millions upon millions. Good for them.

Wealth doesn't automatically equate to greed. In fact, wealth in the hands of a Godly man or woman is a very good thing. Think of all the good that can come from a wealthy person who humbly receives and shares their wealth.

SELFISHNESS

I'm starting to sound like the economist and Wikipedia. Greed, well maybe not greed, but at least a strong individual self-interest appears to run the whole world of commerce. Adam Smith, the father of modern economics, in his book *The Wealth of Nations* calls self-interest the invisible hand of the market setting prices and systems of distribution throughout the world. We've seen the benefits of the invisible hand of self-interest in our mostly capitalistic economic system.

But for the person who wants to please and honor God, isn't self-interest by definition a selfish quality? Shouldn't we be selfless and not selfish. Can you be Godly and act with self-interest?

"Jesus said to his disciples, 'If anyone would come after me, he must deny himself and take up his cross and follow me.'" (Matthew 16:24-28)

"Do nothing out of selfish ambition or vain conceit, but in humility consider others better than yourselves. Each of you should look not only to your own interests, but also to the interests of others. (Philippians 2:3)

"Direct me in the path of your commands, for there I find delight. Turn my heart toward your statutes and not toward selfish gain. (Psalms 119:35-36)

It appears selfishness is frowned upon. In these scriptures, Godly living involves sacrifice for others and sacrifice means denying your self—right?

But what about these other verses?

"The most important one (commandment)," answered Jesus, "is this ... Love the Lord your God with all your heart and with all your soul and with all your mind and with all your strength.' The second is this: 'Love your neighbor as yourself.' There is no commandment greater than these." (Mark 12: 29—31)

We aren't called to love our neighbor and hate ourselves, or love our neighbors and ignore ourselves, we are to love our neighbors as ourselves. Loving yourself, a form of self-interest, appears to be a given. It's stated as though it's something normal—it should come naturally.

"In this same way, husbands ought to love their wives as their own bodies. He who loves his wife loves himself. After all, no one ever hated his own body, but he feeds and cares for it, just as Christ does the church—for we are members of his body." (Ephesians 5: 25-30)

Then there is a verse that speaks to the very reason we pursue God in the first place.

"Without faith it is impossible to please God, because anyone who comes to him must believe that he exists and that he rewards those who earnestly seek him." (Hebrew 11:6)

Would we earnestly seek God if he promised to inflict pain on us? Probably not. We seek him because there is reward in it for ourselves. Apparently there is a love of self, a self-interest, that is actually good.

GODLY SELF-INTEREST

So where do we go from here? How do we deal with this tension between denying yet loving ourselves? We all have desires, strong desires—desires for the good of ourselves and desires for the good of others.

To explore the tension between denying and loving self, let's do a little thought experiment.

Consider it a true statement when I say, "You always and only do what you want," (this sounds rather selfish, but stay with me).

I'm afraid it is true. You do always do what you want. Even when you don't feel like it.

When you want a dish of rocky road ice cream, what do you do? You go to the freezer, serve yourself, and then eat it. So you did what you wanted. This is a true statement (and actually too obvious).

But what if you wanted the rocky road ice cream, had none in the freezer, and had no money to buy some? The only way to fulfill your stomach's desire might be to go to a store and steal it. So how much do you want it? You are awfully fond of rocky road ice cream.

Do you go to the store and steal it? No! And why? Because you didn't want to. Instead, you actually wanted to avoid the morally repugnant act of stealing. So you made a choice, and again you did what you wanted.

Finally, suppose an armed man approached you and gave you the terrible choice between stealing some rocky road ice cream for him or getting shot? This guy really likes rocky road ice cream. You are now faced with a different moral dilemma: steal or die. Either way you win and you lose, but in either case you will do what you want. If you steal the ice cream, you did what you wanted, and avoided getting shot. And if you don't steal the ice cream, you again did what you wanted, but you are now dead.

So in some strange way, we always seek our own self-interest—even when it is sacrificial. Martyrs preferred life I'm sure, but they chose and sacrificed their lives. They did what they wanted, even though it was a selfless act.

The line between selfishness and selflessness can sometimes get blurry. We can do what we want, even though it may be for others or for a higher calling. I can chose to love my neighbor and love myself without being selfish.

In fact, read Ephesians 5 carefully: "He who loves his wife loves himself. After all, no one ever hated his own body, but he feeds and cares for it, just as Christ does the church—for we are members of his body."

The verse says, he who loves his wife is actually loving himself at the same time. The verse also says we are members of the same body, Christ's body. When you are members of the same body, what happens to one happens to the other at the same time. Whatever you do, you do for both of you. There appears to be some mysterious, symbiotic relationship here. By doing something for someone else we are actually doing something for ourselves at the same time.

Now lets look at self-interest mathematically.

"Two are better than one because they have a good return for their labor. For if either of them falls, the one will lift up his companion. But woe to the one who falls when there is not another to lift him up. Furthermore, if two lie down to-gether they keep warm, but how can one be warm. And if one can overpower him who is alone, two can resist him. A cord of three (strands) is not quickly torn apart." (Ecclesiastes 4:9-12)

When two men or women are working together, they can get more accomplished than when working by themselves. They are safer, they are happier, they are more productive. Instead of 1 + 1 = 2, when you work together it is 1 + 1 = 3 or 5. It's a known economic principal—production by multiples.

Actually, it is in your own interest to have another's in-terests in mind. By loving his wife, the husband is actually loving himself. By working together in a group or a family or a whole society, we are actually helping ourselves—we all benefit, everyone with a bit of self-interest.

GREED AND IDOLATRY

So now that we have an understanding that there is such a thing as a healthy, and Godly self-interest, what turns self-interest into greed? And what turns greed into idolatry?

"Put to death, therefore, whatever belongs to your earthly nature: sexual immorality, impurity, lust, evil desires and greed, which is idolatry." (Colossians 3:5)

Greed, in the truest sense, is the extreme of self-interest—not self-interest with the inclusion of others, but self-interest to the exclusion of others. "I want it and I don't want anyone else to have it!"

The word greed is very closely tied to the word covet, as in "Thou shall not covet thy neighbor's (you fill in the blank)." Coveting implies an irresponsible desire—desire gone wild.

Desiring something or someone, or anything this much, is to value it above everything else. Desiring money to this extreme is to value it above things that ought to be more valuable—your family, your friends or your love for God. And when you value a thing and place it above God, you have created by definition an idol. By valuing money or your girl-friend or your career more than God, you have done nothing less than what the Israelites did when they carved a golden calf in the desert and worshiped it. You have created an idol. Greed is actually idolatry wrapped in economic terms.

THE GREEDY TEST

How do we know when we are greedy? How do I know if I value something more than I ought? It's not as hard to tell as you may think.

What do you desire more, money or Godliness? When faced with a choice between the two, do you give up the money easily or do you sweat and consider lying, cheating, or skirting the truth to hold onto the money? When it takes a lot of energy to justify your actions, to hold onto your money or possessions, I'm afraid you may have found an idol.

The rich young man that Jesus recommended selling all he owned made such a choice. He chose his wealth. He valued his idol.

When we are presented with a new job opportunity or anything that could increase our earnings, what are our first thoughts? Is it the things we long to buy with all the extra money we'll earn, or whether it would allow us to do things to please and honor God? Will the new job feed your desire for things, or feed your desire for others and the things that last—the things of God.

There is an old Indian parable about a young brave wrestling with his desire to do what is right.

"Grandfather," the young brave said. "I had a dream last night—a dream that troubled me because it was so real. I dreamed there were two wolves fighting within me. One wolf was good and righteous and the other was evil and deceitful. It was a long bloody fight, and when I woke up I was frightened because it's the same fight I have within me every day.

After a long silence the young brave asked, "Grandfather? Which wolf is going to win?"

The wise old grandfather told him, "The one you feed."

Our hearts are pulled and our desires are drawn in two opposite directions – the things of the world or the things of God—we must make a choice.

JD Rockefeller, the wealthiest man in the United States, the Bill Gates and Warren Buffett of his time said, "I have made millions, but they have brought me no happiness."

John Jacob Astor, the first multimillionaire in the United States in the early 1800s said, "I am the most miserable man on earth."

Henry Ford, the founder of Ford Motor Company said, "I was happier when I was doing a mechanic's job."

"Whoever loves money never has money enough; whoever loves wealth is never satisfied with his income. ... As goods increase, so do those who consume them. And what benefit are they to the owner except to feast his eyes on them?" (Ecclesiastes 5:10-11)

FOUR DESIRES

Greed is not a product of business or money, and to some extent it can't be attributed to self-interest. Greed is a product of our desires—we want, we covet, we desire. Eastern philosophers would say, the problem is desire itself—that we desire at all—and our goal is to overcome all desire. But contrary to their belief, desire is actually a good thing. It's the nature of our desire that's the problem. A whole-hearted desire for what is good is a good thing.

There are four basic desires discussed in scripture, and whether they are good or bad depends on your heart.

"Do not love the world or anything in the world. If anyone loves the world, the love of the Father is not in him. For everything in the world—the cravings of sinful man, the lust of his eyes, and the boasting of what he has and does—comes not from the Father but from the world. The world and its desires pass away, but the man who does the will of God lives forever." (1John 2:15-17).

These verses describe three of our desires, the very strong worldly desires, or lusts—the lust of the flesh, the lust of the eyes and the boastful pride of life.

There's the craving or lust of the flesh—a physical desire for worldly pleasure (as apposed to Godly pleasure). In it you don't want to eat dinner, you absolutely love the act of satisfying your taste buds with food. You don't just want to hear the music, you revel in going to the bar and altering your senses with "mood enhancers." And as your senses grow dull, it takes more food, louder music, and more sensory enhancing substances to satisfy. You have a deep seeded need and you try to fill it by satisfying your senses.

There's the lust of the eyes. When you see a beautiful woman or man, you daydream of their body and possessing him or her in your bedroom. When you see the latest version of your favorite car, you visualize yourself in the driver's seat and long to own one. When you see someone else with the thing you desire (a home, a wife or husband, a career), you feel jealous and resentful. You have a deep seeded need, and you try to fill it by dreaming of how life could be if you only had ...

Then there's the lust of pride. You always look at others in comparison to yourself—with you being financially, athletically, intellectually, or spiritually superior. When you are successful, your first thoughts are of how well you did, rather than acknowledging with gratefulness the work of those who were integral to the success. You have a deep seeded need and you try to fill it with self esteem, your abilities, and your successes.

If you strongly desire the worldly side of the flesh, the eyes, and pride, then (as the verse says) there is no way can experience God's love—the love of God is not in you.

Now let me propose a fourth desire. Let's call it the strong desire, a positive lust, the delight to know and understand God. It is the whole hearted and humble desire to please and honor him. You have a deep seeded need Blasé Pascal would call "the God shaped void," and you fill it by searching out God and knowing his character. When you have this desire it completely transforms the first three.

"Delight yourself in the Lord and he will give you the desires of your heart." (Psalms 37:4)

"As the deer pants for streams of water, so my soul desires you, O God. My soul thirsts for God, for the living God." (Psalms 42:1-2)

The first three desires are all about you. The fourth one moves the other three beyond you to others. The first three lusts are destructive. The last one heals, and when you desire to know God with your whole and humble heart, the other desires are transformed.

When you love God your physical desires of the flesh are completely different. You still get hungry, but now you can sit and enjoy a delicious full meal with friends and family. You still enjoy music, but now you don't need any enhancers.

When you are loving God, you can look at the beautiful form of a naked woman and not lust after her with your eyes, but show Godly compassion by covering her with your coat. When you see a friend driving the new car, or living in the new house you would love to live in, you're sincerely happy for them, not jealous.

And finally, when you love God with your whole and humble heart, you understand that you are uniquely and wonderfully made with special gifts and abilities, without having to compete or compare yourself to others—a Godly pride, with gratefulness.

William Wilberforce used his fortune and wisdom to abolish the slave trade in nineteenth century England. Before spending it on such a Godly cause—abolishing the abduction, mistreatment, and selling of humans—these were his thoughts on our God given desires: "Christianity proposes not to extinguish our natural desires. It promises to bring the desires under control and direct them to their true object."

Greed is most definitely a strong desire, a coveting for things of the world. But with a heart for God—a desire to know, understand, please and honor him—your desires are transformed for the things of God and the ways of Godliness.

10
Money, Leverage and Tools

"There is so much said about money in scripture that there must have been something very important about it. There are twice as many verses about money than there are about faith and prayer—combined. And they are not all warnings about the "eeevils of money." Randy Alcorn Money, Possession and Eternity.

"Money has never made man happy, nor will it, there is nothing in its nature to produce happiness. The more of it one has the more one wants." Benjamin Franklin

"The almighty dollar bequeathed to a child is an almighty curse. No man has the right to handicap his son with such a burden as great as wealth." Andrew Carnegie, 19th century industrialist, billionaire

"Find out how much God has given you and from it take what you need; the reminder is needed by others." St. Augustine, theologian, Bishop of Hippo 4th century

MAGIC PAPER AND ELECTRIC PULSES

I have a confession to make. When I was very young, around 10ish, I had a small square wooden box I kept under my bed. It held all my money. There couldn't have been more than nine dollar bills, a few quarters, and a big silver half dollar in it. On long bored summer days I would pour the money out across my bed, revel in its existence and smell the dollar bills. I was rich!

Since then my affection for money has changed as well as my understanding of it. The idea of money grows more mysterious to me every day, and I say the idea of money because I actually don't see it anymore. I have a few dollar bills in my pocket but they are there only for emergencies. Instead, I use credit cards for everything and allow the Visa folks to track my expenses.

Here's my question: Why in the world would anyone exchange something useful like clothing, food, or a computer, for something as cheap as a piece of colored paper or the swipe of a piece of plastic? At least coins are made of silver or copper metal that have value (although I recently heard it costs around two cents to fabricate one copper penny).

A few years ago I used to receive a magical piece of paper every two weeks signed by my boss with some numbers printed on it. I would drive to the bank and they would take my piece of paper (my payroll check) and input the amount on their company database called my bank account.

Nowadays, I don't even see the piece of paper. I just receive electronic pulses from my company's computer to my bank's computer (direct deposit) and the numbers in my bank account increase automatically. This is great stuff, but does that mean I've just exchanged two weeks of sweat and toil for a few milliseconds of electronic pulses? I think I've been robbed!

If we're going to be shrewd and understand the world we live in, we most definitely need to understand the thing that makes the world go round—money.

THE HISTORY OF MONEY

I've done my homework and found that there's no big warehouse full of thousand dollar bills accounting for all the money in circulation around our country. There is no big room full of gold or silver bullion to cover all our money (at one time there was $147 billion in gold at Fort Knox when there are $900 billion US dollars circulating around the world). There are some big money stashes, but mostly our money exists as electronic pulses tabulated in electronic storage sites and web data banks.

How did we get here? And even more frightening, how in the world does this monetary system work if there is nothing we can touch or feel?

To explain money and the monetary system, lets travel back in time—way back. Computer chips were invented in the late 1950s, the telephone in the late 1800s. Before that we communicated by letter carrier, snail-mail, and it took days if not weeks to get a message. Traveling further back we have George Washington and the beginnings of the USA (1776). Guttenberg's press, Galileo's telescope, Michelangelo's statue of David (1400s), Popes, the Crusades (1000—I wish they never happened). Then Jesus and his disciples (around 30 A.D.). Then to Israeli captivity (500 B.C.), the actual king David himself (1000 B.C.), the Pharaohs, Abraham (1800 B.C.), then Babylon (3000 B.C.) and finally we land in the middle of no where—the agrarian and nomadic life (say 4,000 B.C.).

If you lived way back then, what would you own? Probably just the one piece of clothing you were wearing at the time. There is no money, just you, your family, the goats and land you live on. You can't say you own the land since there is no record of purchase and no king or army to enforce your claim anyway.

If your family had been wise, you probably have a farm that grows everything you need to exist—food from your garden, trees for firewood, mud for shelter, and animals to eat and whose skins make your clothing. Thank you God that I live in the 21st century!

And that's pretty much the way it was for centuries—live, have babies, grow your family, grow our farms and herds, and hardly interact with anyone outside the family.

But let's say one day a nomad travels by and he is covered in the most amazing clothing. It's made of colored fabric and not skins. It's cool—both literally and figuratively—and you would like some of it; What do you do?

I guess you could kill the nomad and take it, but you're a Godly person and want to treat people the way you would like to be treated. So you strike up a conversation and hear the nomad is going to the mountains where it's cold, and he would like something to keep him warm. Suddenly a strange idea comes to you. "I could trade him my hot hairy animal skins for his cool colorful cloth," (very shrewd yet innocent thinking, by the way).

And with this simple but profound idea, the entire world of economics and commerce opens up. You have invented the bartering system. You've traded one commodity for another—skins for cloth. You are the Leonardo DaVinci, the Albert Einstein of your time, and the world will never be the same.

BARTERING

Fast forward now in our story to a time when bartering has become commonplace. The fruits of your idea and the creative nature of people have taken bartering to a new level. Some people are now farmers only, growing vegetables, and leaving the care of animals to other people who are ranchers and shepherds. Farmers no longer need to do ranching since they trade vegetables for meat all the time. In fact, your nomadic friend's family have gone exclusively into making colorful cloth. They're very good at it and now rely on cloth making for their livelihood. Their security, their food, depend on trading with the farmers and shepherds. You've created your own little economic civilization. And because each family can focus on the thing they do best, they get better and better at it and grow more efficient. And with efficiency comes profit. And with profit they can buy other things, some niceties like a vacation cruise on the Nile, or they may choose to give some of it away to the needy.

Then one day while on vacation your friends, the fabric family, see something beautiful as they tour the Nile. They spot someone making jewelry out of a special shiny metal, and they want to bring some home to show the relatives. Since they loaded up some spare cloth for their vacation, they make a trade.

Once they show the jewelry to their friends in their home town, they want some for themselves. Not because they are greedy, but because they like it, it gives them pleasure, and just like the fabric family, they trade their surplus vegetables or meat for it.

Suddenly your mind races to your ancestors who changed the face of the world with the idea of bartering. And you have an epiphany. "Everyone likes this metal stuff. It's small so I can divide it up, hide and transport it easily. What if I use these pieces of metal to trade for a lot of different things? Instead of traveling with my sheep or vegetables or cloth, I could float down the Nile with this metal and use it to trade."

METAL MONEY

Well, you get the picture. Something that everyone saw as valuable and easily dividable began to be used as a substitute for raw bartering—the first real money.

Creative people over the centuries have used many forms of money. Egyptians used gold bars as a medium of exchange as far back as the Pharaohs. At one time salt was very valuable because it could preserve food over long periods of time, and it could be easily divided into various quantities. In ancient Rome, soldiers were paid with salt, not gold, leading to the statement used in some circles today, "He is not worth his salt"—meaning the soldier is not worth what he was paid.

In the British colony of New South Wales, rum was the medium of exchange instead of gold or silver. But one of the most common forms of exchange was precious metal. Eventually gold and silver pieces were used in more standard weights and coinage became the common form of money.

But as coins became more popular and families became more prosperous, another problem sprang up. They found that coins were also easy to steal (easier than a goat or bushel of vegetables). So another inventive young person had the idea to warehouse money for safe keeping and formed the first bank.

Early banks were located in temples and palaces where people were constantly around, and the risks of robbery were limited. You would bring your gold or other valuable commodities, give them to the banker and the banker would in turn give you a note, a hand written piece of paper, stating what you had deposited in the bank. If you ever wanted your gold, you would present your bank note back to the banker.

PAPER MONEY

It's only a logical step from this to paper money. Once you had a slip of paper, a banknote, if you wanted to buy something, instead of going back to the bank, picking up your gold, traveling under the threat of theft, and giving the heavy gold to your trading partner (who would then travel back to his bank and deposit it there), you could just sign over your banknote. So banknotes became a preferred form of exchange—the first bank checks.

Soon coinage and banknotes became more widespread, but as you would think something sprang up to cheat the system. Creative little artists found they could make identical copies of the coins and paper notes and the art of counterfeiting developed. So to combat this problem, special presses and stamps were made and the king's image was stamped on the money to make them harder to counterfeit and safer to trade.

Then not too long afterward the image on the money became what made the money trustworthy—not the weight of metal or the bank it represented. The image of the king that protected the money was more important than the weight of the metal. Coins eventually were no longer valued by their weight. If it had the stamp of the king or emperor on it and the coin said it was worth 20 shekels, pounds, or cents, then that was what it was worth, no matter how heavy it was. If you were going to trade in that country, you would use the approved money.

Look at a bill in your wallet. It states: "This note (banknote) is legal, tender for all debts, public and private." It is issued by a bank run by the U.S. and backed by the government. It was printed by your government and is lawful, nay required, to be used in trade in the U.S.

Nowadays, with the use of credit cards for everything from candy to cars, we no longer even use banknotes or checks. But who really cares. A check is just a piece of paper that represents a number on a database at the bank anyway.

Our money is no longer backed by gold on deposit in a bank somewhere, it's backed by the faith and credit of the U.S. government, who relies on you and me, going on our merry way, exchanging our work and goods for a piece of paper or a number in a database that everyone promises to accept. You can complain about money and the lack of backing of the dollar, but it has worked well as our mode of exchange for decades (without anyone knowing the details) and should in the future—as long as the governmental guys with the multiple PhDs keep a watchful eye on it. Our money has turned into a simple electronic scorecard in the competition of work. If you trade well, you get a higher score, if you don't, your score goes down.

I apologize if I sound a bit cynical. We have recently gone

through a very deep recession where faith in our economic system has lowered everyone's score—we gambled (some without knowing) and lost, for the moment.

MONEY AND MORALITY

Is this monetary system morally wrong? It does sound rather tenuous—like a house of cards ready to be blown over by the slightest doubt in our government's ability to maintain it.

Although there are a lot of possibilities for moral failure in the printing and maintenance of our monetary system (because people are involved with different motives), money is just a tool, similar to a plow or a wheel. Tools are used to increase productivity—just like a plow can increase the crop yielded by a single farmer, money increases trade by making it faster and more convenient.

Scripture actually encourages the use of money. Back when the rural Israelites had to travel to offer their sacrifices in the Temple, God recommended (Deuteronomy 14:24-26) they trade their crops or livestock for money so they could travel more easily. They would then use the money to buy other grain or livestock upon their arrival. The intent was to offer a sacrifice, giving of your work in thanks to God, not the hassle of traveling with it.

Why we use our money is what is important. Why we use something is what makes it morally significant. Since money can be exchanged for almost anything, it holds the keys to both tempt us and afford us enjoyment. It's both a potent drop of poison and a stem cell of life at the same time.

The focus of our lives should not be on the things we compile over our life time because those things don't last. They are easily stolen or broken.

"Do not store up for yourselves treasures on earth, where moth and rust destroy, and where thieves break in and steal. But store up for yourselves treasures in heaven, where moth and rust do not destroy, and where thieves do not break in and steal. For where your treasure is, there your heart will be also." (Matthew 6:19-21)

Jesus was saying the Godly life is a thing of the heart. In this verse he was in essence asking, "What is it that you treasure—your family, your bank account, heaven?"

Do you want to know where your heart is? Look where you spend your treasure. When you earn a few extra bucks, what is the first thing that comes to mind, "Wow, now I can go snow skiing." Or do you say, "Thank you God for the cash, what do want me to do with it?" (You might be surprised. God did make the snow).

Dr. Richard Halverson is quoted, "Money is an exact index to a man's true character. All through scripture there is an intimate correlation between the development of a man's character and how he handles his money."

Look at your credit card statement or checkbook. Where is your heart? Of course you need to pay your bills and eat, but where does any other money go? It may be time for a spiritual course correction.

MONEY AND GIVING

You can spend your money on things that can rust or be stolen, but on the other side of the spectrum you can use your money for Godly things—providing good things for your family, neighbor, or providing for your church or a non-profit ministry, providing for those who need your money.

Paul says to his friends at the church in Corinth, "Remember this: Whoever sows sparingly will also reap sparingly, and whoever sows generously will also reap generously. Each man should give what he has decided in his heart to give, not reluctantly or under compulsion, for God loves a cheerful giver." (2 Corinthians 9:6-7)

Have you ever felt guilty for not giving enough? Why is that?

I would like to recommend something controversial. Love God, and give what you want to give—large, small, or nothing. Love God, and give because you want to and what you want to. And over time, my bet is your heart will begin to change, and you will begin to know the freedom God desires for those who love him. And as your love and thankfulness to God grows, you will most likely want to give because you have grown to love him and his people in need. Then you'll understand what Paul meant when he talked about sowing and reaping—the joy of giving with great returns on investment.

Randy Alcorn, a pastor, in his book *Money, Possession and Eternity* said, "I have found that cheerful givers love God and love him more deeply each time they give. To me, one of the few experiences comparable to the joy of leading someone to Christ is the joy of making wise and generous choices with my money and possessions. Both are supreme acts of worship. Both are exhilarating. Both are what we are made for."

SHREWD MONEY

Have you ever wondered why the edges of our coins have ridges on them? Before the mints started ribbing the edges of coins, some creative thieves would shave the precious metal from the perimeter of the coin and sell the shavings for extra money. The ribs allowed banks to know whether someone was shaving the money.

Ever since money was invented, men have been shrewd in handling it—shrewd, but not necessarily innocent. Countries have influenced the value of another country's money by buying large quantities (taking it out of circulation). The goldsmiths, as mentioned earlier, exchanged their client's gold for banknotes. But some slyly handed out more bank notes than the amount of gold stored in their vault. Crafty little guys, weren't they?

When we buy and sell things, using money as a tool, a go-between for exchange, everything is fine. When we get into the money business (trading, lending, and creating money) the system moves into a different world. The moral principle at issue is just and fair trade. God is just, he delights in justice, and so should we. God does not like injustice, and neither should we.

"Use honest scales and honest weights, an honest ephah (a bushel) and an honest hin (a gallon)." (Leviticus 19:36)

"The Lord abhors dishonest scales, but accurate weights are his delight." (Proverbs 11:1)

"The merchant uses dishonest scales; he loves to defraud." (Hosea 12:7)

There's little that's new in the world of business. Back in biblical times crafty merchants and lenders were shrewd with the monetary system, but definitely not innocent. They would use one set of weights on their scales for one person and another set for another—the bottom line was that they were dishonest. Even Jesus was uncharacteristically harsh with dishonest traders and money lenders when it came to taking advantage of people.

"When it was almost time for the Jewish Passover, Jesus went up to Jerusalem. In the temple courts he found men selling cattle, sheep, and doves, and others sitting at tables exchanging money. So he made a whip out of cords, and drove all from the temple area, both sheep and cattle; he scattered the coins of the money changers and overturned their tables. To those who sold doves he said, 'Get these out of here! How dare you turn my Father's house into a market!" (John 2:13-16)

The buying and selling of sacrificial animals wasn't a problem. In fact, it was recommended to those who were going on a long trip—sell sheep for money, travel to temple, buy sheep to sacrifice—it's easier. The problem wasn't commerce, the problem was injustice. Wouldn't you get angry with someone taking advantage of a soul on a spiritual pilgrimage? I picture the Temple market full of haggling: "I'm sorry sir, but you sold your lamb for $10 pieces of silver at home, but sheep are scarce here in Jerusalem. I can get you a lamb for $100. Take it or leave it."

The problem wasn't with money or animals. The problem was the manipulation of value—taking advantage of supply and demand, weights and measures. Money is just a tool for exchange. But in the hands of wolves, the tool is used with wrong motives, with greedy, covetous hearts, with the intent of taking advantage of those in need.

MISUNDERSTOOD MONEY

It's strange that something so benign as money can be so misunderstood, but as we've seen, money is much more complicated than it appears. Just as any tool is used to produce more with less effort, leveraging our work to multiply its outcome, money as a tool can be used as a tool with the same multiplying affect. The problem is how we use the tool of money—to multiply the things of God (providing for and encouraging the spiritual and physical needs of a needy world), or the ungodly things of the world (providing for and encouraging those things opposed to the purposes of God).

11

Sales, Marketing and Trust

"Why sell ice to Eskimos when you can sell life jackets to drowning men?" Jack Galloway, Director of Dave Ramsey's Real Estate Resource.

"Any business arrangement that is not profitable to the other person will in the end prove unprofitable for you. The bargain that yields mutual satisfaction is the only one that is apt to be repeated." B. C. Forbes, founder Forbes Magazine

"Let advertisers spend the same amount of money improving their products as they do advertising, and they wouldn't have to advertise it." Will Rogers, American humorist, social commentator

"You might as well praise a man for not robbing a bank." Bobby Jones, legendary golfer replying to praise for telling the truth and assessing himself a penalty stroke at the 1925 U.S. Open.

"The lure of the promised land is that it is 'flowing with milk and honey' (Deauteronomy. 6:3). An adman couldn't have come up with a better strapline." Richard Higginson, from his book, "Questions of Business Life"

SELLING THE TRUTH

"Is it OK to lie?"

That's what I ask my classes at the beginning of the topic

of sales and marketing.

Everyone wags their heads, smiles that they know the easy answer, and say in unison, "No."

Then I follow with, "If I were selling you my car and I told you, 'It runs beautifully,' when I actually knew the engine may break down any day, would that be lying?"

"Yes" everyone responds, although some sly-minded students think they could fudge on this one (it does actually run beautifully until it breaks down), but they eventually agree that this is a lie because I knew it was a lie when I told it.

"What about little white lies?"

If your wife or girlfriend asked you, 'Do these jeans look good on me?' (when in your opinion they really didn't). Would you tell them the truth, or run from the room?

"What about a little exaggeration? That's OK, right? Isn't the entire multibillion advertising industry built on 'just a little exaggeration?'"

The theologian Martin Luther had concerns about lies, but surprisingly he could justify them when the liar's motives were altruistic. "What harm would it do, if a man told a good strong lie for the sake of the good and for the Christian church...a lie out of necessity, a useful lie, a helpful lie, such lies would not be against God, he would accept them."

Clement of Alexander and Origen also said that lies were not wrong when justified.

On the other hand there is St. Augustine who argued the other side saying, "Just lies are like chaste adultery"—there is no such thing as an innocent lie.

No wonder I'm confused. Great theologians don't even agree on the topic.

Unfortunately, when I think of sales and marketing the idea of lies and deception come to mind rather than truth and trust. We are bombarded with commercials, online ads, junk mail, and computer generated sales calls ever day, and as these filter through my mind, all I can think is, "I don't trust these guys. All they want is a quick buck." Thankfully there are people and companies who have a different view of sales and marketing.

Scott Bedbury was the marketing wonder for Nike and Starbucks. In his book *A New Brand World*, Bedbury discusses his advertising philosophy.

"The key in this category is to build on brand trust ... Trust is the heart of any brand. The consensus is that for better or for worse, all the money in the world can't buy you love or trust. You have to earn trust and love by how you behave ..."

Love and trust. Aren't these religious words?

Brand loyalty based on trust is a hard thing to break. Do you trust a celebrity spokesperson? Do you think they would be paid millions to advertise products if you didn't admire (a form of love) and trust him (a form of faith)?

TRUST

We Americans live in the epitome of the consumer society. Advertising is everywhere – on every web page, along every highway, interrupting our favorite programming, even in the bathroom stall. My wife and I no longer answer our home phone because more times than not the person calling is selling something under the guise of a survey. Trust is a rare commodity in today's world of commerce.

When my family travels to an unfamiliar place and hunger grips our stomachs, we don't consider dropping into any local dive for dinner. Who knows whether the place had just reopened from health department violations. Instead we go to a place we are familiar with, a place we have dined in the past that has consistently met our dining expectations—a place we trust.

Even Albert Einstein's wife Elsa said, "I don't understand my husband's theory of relativity, but I know my husband, and I know he can be trusted."

Trust requires three important ingredients—familiarity, transparency, and consistency over time.

Trust is a quality that is not quickly gained and can be lost in a second. It's the close cousin of integrity. Trust requires at least some familiarity. Who automatically trusts someone they know nothing about? No wonder companies spend millions of dollars on brand management and advertising to familiarize you with themselves or their product. The more familiar you become, the better the possibility to trust them.

When a company or person is trustworthy, they also have a transparency about them—they want people to see that they are accountable. If something goes wrong, instead of hiding behind a barrage of words (as my favorite politicians do) or creating a confusing argument (as my favorite lawyers do), they strive to make the truth simple, clear, and understood.

When I first met my wife, all I knew of her was that she was beautiful and kind. But the closer we became and the more I saw that her kindness was genuine; that she wouldn't compromise her values when faced with hardship, and that she was quick to admit when she failed—the more transparent she was—the more I trusted her. I didn't trust her because she was perfect, I trusted her because she was transparent.

Consistency is another element of trust. Like a science experiment, when you get the same result over and over again, you trust you'll have the same outcome in the future. When you go to a certain restaurant or take your car to a certain mechanic and their quality is consistent each time you return, you trust them.

You can even trust a thief. The more a detective becomes familiar with their work, the more transparent his actions are, and when he acts consistently over a long period of time, these trustworthy traits can be used to apprehend him.

LIES AND DECEPTION

Unfortunately lies and deception have become part of the normal course of business. From selling broken used cars to an assistant simply telling someone on the phone that the boss is not in (when he is standing next to her), lies and deception have become lazy crutches and an easy excuse to make a sale. So let's dive into the world of lies to understand what happens to the truth and trust when lies arc employed.

Lies and deception are actually slightly different things. Lying is stating something that is not true (something contrary to reality). Deceit on the other hand is more sinister than lying. Deceit involves the desire to manipulate—telling a lie to influence someone to do something. I could lie and say, "I worked for the President," to make me look good, but if I tell the same lie to get a job, it moves into the world of deceit.

I don't think there is a society in the world, religious or not, that condones deceit. It's a universal moral code—every one knows we ought to tell the truth and ought not deceive. Even a thief and a murderer expects the truth from their partners in crime.

"Wherefore, putting away lying, speak every man truth with his neighbor ..." (Ephesians 4:25).

The wolves are out there doing their best to deceive us, and their deceit can be subtle. In fact, the world of deceit is more common and subtle that you may think.

MUTUALLY ACCEPTED DECEPTION

Alexander Hill, in his book *Just Business,* describes four kinds of deception: mutually accepted, exaggeration, ambiguity, and omission. Let's look at each one of these.

I love movies—the stories, the actors, the photography, and the music. And the thing that amazes me about movies is that I watch them totally buying into their lies and deceit.

The whole movie industry is built on deceit. We even pay money to see it.

When I watch a movie about Adolf Hitler, and someone says, "That guy sure played Hitler well," I don't stand up in outrage and say, "You mean to tell me that wasn't really Adolf Hitler?"

The reason I'm not outraged is that I know it wasn't Hitler, it was an actor playing Hitler. The actor deceived me—making me think he was Hitler. And that's OK. We mutually accept the deceit—the actor knowing he was deceiving me and me knowing he wasn't Hitler. If the actor does a great job the Academy of Motions Pictures will award him an Oscar. This deceiver gets paid and an award too!

Mutually accepted deception is when I know I'm being deceived and the deceiver knows they're deceiving me—and we both accept it.

I was a defensive back in my football days, and the job of a defensive back is to try and keep the quarterback and receivers from doing their job—completing passes. On the other hand, the job of the quarterback and receivers is to complete passes and score touchdowns. During a game, after the center snaps the ball, the receiver starts running at me and looks to the left (as if he is going to run left), but then he suddenly moves his whole body to the right! What a jerk! He deceived me! And just to catch a pass and score a touchdown in a silly game.

But that's part of it. I entered the game knowing it was their intention to deceive. In fact, to put the shoe on the other foot, my intention as a defensive back is to hide the type of coverage before the snap of the ball for the same reason—to deceive them. It's all part of the game. In the world of movies and football everyone knows the rules, or should know them before they get involved.

But be careful. In business the rules are not always so clear and when you start playing with someone unfamiliar with the game, and when you zig when they thought it was your moral obligation to zag, you have the potential of losing that important element of trust.

EXAGGERATION

There's also the deception of exaggeration—the foundation of most advertising campaigns and sales pitches. Some call this is the "no harm, no foul" rule.

When I was very young, I saw a commercial advertising some athletic shoes claiming, "These shoes will make you run faster!" I nagged my mother until she bought me a pair, and as you would expect I was disappointed. I wasn't faster. My sister still outran me.

Unwrap your next hamburger. Does it look like the photo you saw on the commercial or on the drive through menu you ordered from? Do the clothes you purchase make you look like the model who wore them? Of course not. The photo of the hamburger and the model are produced to make them look appealing—exaggerating their good qualities.

Advertisers present what we desire (our dream of reality), not necessarily what the reality is. But when we buy and compare reality (the truth) to the dream—the greater the product strays from the truth, the less we trust future products.

My trust in television advertising was never the same after buying those shoes. Exaggeration may illicit some short term gains (a one time sale or two), but in the long run it erodes trust. And who goes back to do business with someone they don't trust?

AMBIGUITY

Another form of deception is even more subtle, although it can be just as harmful as exaggeration. Instead of speaking the truth, you speak around it. When I think of ambiguity, my mind turns to politicians and lawyers, the masters of spin and ambiguity, but there was a priest who once used it wisely.

Athanasius, a patriarch of the early church at Alexandria, was once pursued by a couple of assassins dispatched by the Roman Emperor. One night as the men approached Athanasius, a man they had never met, they asked him, "Is Athanasius around here?" Athanasius himself answered, "He is not far." And the assassins passed by, continuing their search.

Now that was a shrewd and crafty man! He didn't lie, and he avoided death by being ambiguous.

Abraham, when traveling to Egypt with his beautiful wife Sarah, found himself in a difficult place when the Egyptian men were attracted to her. Abraham was afraid they would kill him to steal his bride, so he told them she was his sister. The deception worked and he was spared because of Abraham's ambiguity. And he actually didn't tell a complete falsehood. Sarah was actually his half-sister. But when Pharaoh found out, he ran them out of the country.

Ambiguity is similar to exaggeration, it may work the first or second time, but over the long term, who trusts someone who doesn't tell you the simple truth.

OMISSION

You'd think that silence would be acceptable, and certainly better than telling an outright lie—but it's not. Remaining quiet seems morally neutral, but sometimes it's wrong to remain silent, and it is our moral duty to speak up.

We should speak up when someone has the right to know. Not everyone has the right to know everything about your business. You may have trade secrets or confidentiality agreements, or you may have good reason to remain silent. But when someone has the right to know, you should speak up.

Could you sell your home to someone without informing them that the foundation was damaged? Could you advertise cigarettes as healthy after research linked them to lung cancer and heart disease? Sometimes we should speak up, but sometimes we should remain silent.

Samuel the prophet was in a dilemma when God asked him to go anoint David, the young son of Jesse, as the new King of Israel. The dilemma was Israel already had a king, Saul, and if Saul knew Samuel was traveling to Bethlehem to find his replacement, Samuel might have been put to death.

As you read the story of Samuel's predicament, you find that God told Samuel to go to do two things. Number one was to go to Bethlehem to offer a sacrifice, because number two, at the ceremony God would show who he had anointed as the next king. But God also told Samuel that, when asked, he was to tell reason number one only and withhold number two (1 Samuel 16:1-3). Withholding the fact that Samuel was going to look for a new king was important to both Samuel and Saul. It allowed Samuel to find the new king David, and it kept Saul from committing murder in a jealous rage.

Not everyone needs to know every reason you do what you do. Some deserve your silence. But when someone has the right to know, you should speak

We should also speak up to avoid harm.

Remaining silent when someone is being harmed unjustly, or when someone is unaware of the harm they are entering into, can be as immoral as any lie.

If you were a nurse, would you speak up when you knew a doctor was about to administer a deadly drug? If a friend were about to step into traffic, unaware of the truck barreling down the street would you remain silent?

The drug manufacturer Ely Lilly created a prescription drug Zyprexa, but several employees noticed the company was fraudulently marketing it. Another pharmaceutical giant Schering-Plough was sued for fraudulent pricing when several of their executives blew the whistle on them. Ely Lilly had to pay $1.4 billion in damages and Schering-Plough paid $300 million, but their illegal and immoral acts would have gone unchecked without someone speaking up.

The final reason we should speak up is because we would want to know if we were in their place. When selling your house, if you would prefer to know that there was a stain on the floor that's hard to find, go ahead and tell them. Tell them everything you'd like to know yourself. It shows a passion for the truth and exposes a life of honesty that screams, "You can trust me." —a trait that points to the kind of person you are— one who delights in kindness, justice and righteousness as God does.

The Golden Rule is the bottom line in most things any-way.We should do for others as we would have them do for us, with the corollary, we should not do to others what we would not want done to us.

CONFLICTS

So far we've been dealing with relatively easy concepts. Be familiar, transparent and consistent over time and you'll be trusted. Avoid harming your integrity with Exaggeration, Ambiguity and Omission. But the world is often more complex than this, and the truth is hard to decipher.

Let's say you were a salesman at a small jewelry store. You've been working there for several years, you're friends, with the manager and have grown to know the jewelry business from the inside out.

One day as you walk to work you notice the jewelry store across the street has a certain watch for sale—at a price 50% lower than the same watch you sell at your store.

After you open your doors, a new customer then walks through the door and begins to eye the watch, so you pull it out and begin the sell.

Here is my question: Would you say to the new customer, "Hey, did you know this exact same watch is on sale for half this price across the street?"

I've posed this question to salesmen, pastors, real estate developers, counselors, and to my surprise, I get different answers. The salesmen and real estate developers don't hesitate a bit. "No way. If they want to buy the watch here, who am I to stop them? Besides I owe my allegiance to my boss, not this new customer."

The pastors and counselors, on the other hand, hesitate before they answer. "If we're supposed to love our neighbors as ourselves—if I were in their shoes—I would want to know. So I would probably tell them." But when I ask what their friend the manager would say, they change their answer. "If I did this, my boss would probably get angry, and since I owe my allegiance to my boss over a stranger, I would feel terrible," so they change their minds and admit they probably wouldn't share the information with the customer.

Then I ask them all, "What if your grandmother, or you daughter came in and looked at the watch? Would you tell them?"

I know love confuses the economic system, but I don't let them off the hook. "Who do you owe your loyalty and allegiance to, your boss who pays your bills or the family member you love?"

Conflicts like this happen all the time. Should I tell the truth or obey my boss when he tells me from his office, "Tell the caller I'm not here." Should I tell the prospective buyer that the company is going out of business and their warranty will not be valid? Do I entertain my client at the adult nightclub he wants to go to?

Some conflicts are more positive, but they are still conflicts. Who do I give my time and moneys to—the church or the independent missionary? Of the three missionaries I want to support, which one do I chose? Who do I want to work for, the local nonprofit or a for-profit company who builds things to serve the community?

Jesus tells of such a predicament. King David found himself hungry while running from the threats of King Saul. David entered the Temple, and asked for food, but the only food left was the sacred showbread that only the priests could use. So the priest had a problem. Does he give him the special showbread that, by law, was to be eaten only by the priests, or does he let him go hungry? It's right to feed a hungry man and it's right to obey the ceremonial laws. Which is more important? Jesus says to feed the hungry and excuses the minor indiscretion of the law for the safety and health of David. (Matthew 12: 1-6)

HOW DO YOU DECIDE

So the question now is, "When I come to a conflict between choosing my boss or my conscience, or between my family and the church, how do I decide?" Which of the conflicting principles do I use?

Remember, we're not trying to decide between a right thing and a wrong thing. This is too obvious—do the right thing. We're talking about the choice between two right things.

Paul gives us insight into the answer. He says that whatever we chose, we should do it in confidence, faith, and peace in our hearts.

When Paul tells the Romans how to decide when there is a conflict between their own preferences and the preferences of others, he says that whatever they decide, "Each one should be fully convinced in his own mind... Blessed is the man who does not condemn himself... But the man who has doubts is condemned ... everything that does not come from faith is sin." (Romans 14:5-23)

Paul isn't talking about sins like murder or theft here, he's talking about preferences and choices, of faith and confidence—but he still calls it sin. I find it interesting how important it is to be convinced that you are doing the right thing. If you aren't convinced, Paul equates such a lack of faith to the worldly, evil, and rebellious world of sin.

Paul also says when making such decisions it also requires an inner peace. Our heart, our honest inner motives and intentions, can be the most important factors in such decisions.

"Let the peace of Christ rule in your hearts..." (Colossians 3:15)

The Apostle John references the same idea, "Dear friends, if our hearts do not condemn us, we have confidence before God ... because we obey his commands and do what pleases him." (1 John 3:2122)

If we do anything, we should do it in confidence and the inner peace that it is what God wants us to do. If we don't have this confidence and peace, we are acting on something other than Godly faith. When your boss tells you to tell someone he is not in his office, you might do it the first time (out of respect for your boss), but later, with humility and without judgment, you should express your concerns that telling anyone a lie, even a little white lie, goes against what you stand for as a follower of Christ. Ask how to solve the problem in a way that gives you confidence that God would be pleased. Then you can answer the phone and serve your boss with a clear conscience, in confidence and good faith.

That's how you can do, "whatever you do, whether in word or deed, do it all in the name of the Lord Jesus, giving thanks to God the Father through him." (Colossians 3:17)

When you walk by the competitor's sign selling your watch for 50% off, and a question raises in your mine, "What will I do if a customer sees that sign?" You should pursue peace and confidence. You should go directly to the manager and ask, "What should I do?" Then you can go about your business walking in the faith that you can please and honor God and your boss in everything you do. Do what it takes so our heart doesn't condemn you and your conscience is clear.

THE GOAL OF TRUST

What does all this have to do with sales, marketing, and trust? It has plenty to do with it. Showing yourself trustworthy is an extension of the character of God.

The entirety of sales and marketing can be wrapped up in one word—communication. You can communicate with passion and clarity for hours, but if your customer doesn't receive it—no sale. Then in the next sentence you can communicate very poorly, and the person gets it—and you close the deal.

God himself did a little sales and marketing when motivating Israel to go to the promised land.

"And I have promised to bring you up out of your misery in Egypt into the land of the Canaanites ... a land flowing with milk and honey." (Exodus 3:17)

Wouldn't you want to travel to such a place after being a slave, then roaming around the desert for 40 years? The dream of this place would keep me going.

TRUST, BELIEF, FAITH—THEY ARE THE SAME WORDS.

"Without faith it is impossible to please God, because anyone who comes to him must believe that he exists and that he rewards those who earnestly seek him." (Hebrews 11:6)

Who would believe scripture if it were proved untrustworthy? No wonder so much energy is spent on any possible disconnect between scripture and geology (the origin and age of the universe), anthropology (the origin and age of species), and archeology (the historic records of the past). Our trust in God and his revelation to us through scripture is at stake—and rightfully so.

I think those who don't trust scripture aren't familiar with it. Upon first picking it up, they don't know why all the books are organized the way they are, who wrote them and why, and the interrelationship of all its characters.

The more I delve headlong into the Bible, and the more familiar I become with it, the more transparent the actions of a kind, just, and righteous God become. The acts of God become more consistent. And as I trust scripture more and more, the more I trust in the God who chose to reveal himself through it.

A Godly person in the sales and marketing business communicates the way God would communicate—offering the truth about their product with a view toward a long term trusted relationship.

There is no use for playing on a customer's lust for things, their fears of loss, or to entice their hearts with greed. "Trust" and "Trustworthiness" are invaluable traits in the world of sales and marketing and I don't think it's any accident that they are some of the traits intrinsic with God's character. Would we seek God if he weren't trustworthy.

Trust is no light thing, it is the very foundation of any relationship—between you and God, between you and your neighbors, and to those to whom you sell.

12

Negotiations, Price and Values

"You don't get what you deserve. You get what you negotiate." Dr. Chester L. Karrass, author and chairman of the largest negations training organization in the world

"Ever wonder about those people who spend $2 apiece on those little bottles of Evian water? Try spelling Evian backward." George Carlin, comedian, social critic

"If you don't get what you want, it's a sign either that you did not seriously want it, or that you tried to bargain over the price." Rudyard Kipling, British author and poet

"Man is an animal that makes bargains: no other animal does this—no dog exchanges bones with another." Adam Smith, first author of modern economics

"People that value its privileges above its principles soon lose both." Dwight D. Eisenhower, five-star general and Supreme Commander of Allied forces during WWII, President 1952-1960

TO MARKET TO MARKET TO BUY

Few things are more fascinating to me than the marketplace. It's the barometer of a culture's values expressed by their purchases. In other words, we buy what we value and our values are what define our culture. Trillions of dollars of things and non-things (goods and services) change hands each year. In the US alone we spent more than $700 million on deodorant and skin creams and billions more on advice from our accountants, lawyers, psychologists. Creative people are paid millions to design the look of a new car or bar of soap, and millions more are spent advertising the product (a 30-second commercial spot during the Super Bowl costs over $2 million).

For me, the genius award goes to the packagers of bottled water. Prior to 1977 when Perrier launched a $5 million campaign to sell a beautifully designed bottle of water (the liquid you can find easily at your sink), water was sold only as mineral or carbonated water (bubbly water). Before Perrier's campaign 300,000 bottles were sold annually, but by 1997 more than 3 million bottles of water were sold with titles from Evian to Ozarka to Sierra Springs. The big bottlers of soft drinks couldn't help but get on the bandwagon as Coke and Pepsi joined in with Dasani and Aquafina.

As much as I can understand the convenience and health benefits of having a bottle of water next to you instead of a soft drink, it still amazes me that we pay from $1 to $5 for something that is almost free from your faucet at home or from the water fountain in every public building in the country—look for them, they are near the public restrooms—I know, I'm an architect, building codes require them.

NEGOTIATIONS AND PRICE

We in the U.S. are far removed from the rest of the world when it comes to negotiations. We hardly negotiate for anything. But go to a market in third world countries and the price quoted by the seller is almost never the price you pay. It's part of the lively interplay of haggling. It's part of the fun. But move into the refined palaces of shopping—boutiques and department store—and no one considers haggling over the price of a bottle of perfume or diamonds (although negotiations are actually going on behind the scenes).

Back home as you walk down the aisles of your local grocery store looking for your favorite cereal, you pass rows and rows of boxes with loud colorful packaging all screaming at you, "Buy me!" Then as you find your favorite, you just pick it up and put it in your cart, walk through the check-out stand and you're on your way home. But let's say one day, as you realized your pocket book was wearing thin, you eyed the generic brand of cereal that sold for 25% less. You decide to pass on your normal brand and give the new one a try—and you like it, "Hey Mikey!" You then decide to stop buying your normal brand, and without knowing it you've fired the initial shot of the negotiating war for your breakfast cereal.

If everyone chooses like you, the manufacturer of your original favorite cereal will get the news (by the sales figures from the grocer) and negotiate back. They may offer more cereal in the box, or give you a prize or coupon. They may even lower the price to match the generic brand—upon which the generic brand may lower their price, and the negotiations continue.

A store is not doing us a favor by putting their merchandise on sale. Sales are just a way to get you into the store to buy things you negotiated to a lower price by purchasing something else.

Negotiations is not an immoral game of haggling. Negotiating is very simply determining the value of something.

It's simple because the value of most things is just the price we are willing to pay. If the shoes are too expensive for our taste, we say it by not buying them. If the same shoes were on sale at half the price, we still may not value them enough to make the trade. However, if we hear the manufacturer plans on donating one pair of shoes to those in need for every pair we buy, something else may trigger in our minds to value these shoes over others, and we may part with our money. We valued them not just for their price but for other personal reasons. It's that simple. We buy (trade our money for) things we value. When we buy we negotiate.

I never liked the word negotiate. To me it's the combination of two words—negative and irritate. Who enjoys the tension of haggling except for a few aggressive types who grew up arguing as a daily norm? But negotiate we do, every day, whether we know it or not.

THE VALUE OF THINGS AND NON-THINGS

How much is something worth?

Economists would say something is worth what a motivated buyer and a motivated seller agree on for a trade. The final value of any thing is what Joe the supplier is willing to accept and what Sue the buyer is willing to pay.

When it comes to price, it may not matter how much Joe spent to get the product to the market (research and development, purchase of raw materials and equipment to build the thing). Of course Joe would want to recoup his costs and make a profit to boot, but if Sue doesn't see the value in it, he may have to sell his product for a loss. It happens all the time.

How much are you worth? And I don't mean the value of your weight in body parts. I mean what value does your company place on your employment, in other words how much are you paid? When a prospective employer makes you an offer, do you just accept it, or do you shop around and negotiate a for a better value? You may be surprised how much flexibility there is in your salary. The more value you bring to a company through sales, connections, experience, or hard work, the more value a company has to share with you.

How valuable is justice? When the police catch a murderer and the evidence to convict him is lacking, do they go to court with the possibility of the murderer being acquitted for lack of evidence, or do they negotiate a plea bargain to get the criminal off the streets? Serious negotiations go on like this every day—it's not always a lovely picture.

My clients don't pay me for manufacturing anything, they pay me for something invisible—my expertise and advice. I call this a non-thing. I've actually convinced some people that my advice is worth paying for—who knew? I guess my education, experience and other skills are worth something. I supply what they want and we've negotiated a fee for it.

I once had a discussion with an employee about and how medical doctors can justify charging so much for their services. Her reasoning for their high cost of services (over, say, the services of a plumber or architect) was that they spent long years in specialized education and internship prior to becoming a practicing physician. And although I agreed that doctors have sacrificed a great deal for their education and position, I didn't agree that it was their education and position that allowed them to charge more for their services. The reason was the supply of doctors was relatively low and the need for their services was relatively high.

If there were 1,000 doctors in a small town and 1,000 patients with a choice, the competition among the doctors would drive some away and others to lower their fees. And in the reverse, if there was one doctor in town and 1,000 patients in need of the operation, the doctor could name his price (although his conscience and moral compass would affect his decisions).

It's true that there are fewer doctors and architects and accountants in the marketplace because they are difficult professions, but there are also laws that protect the public from those trying to practice medicine without training. These laws and their professional associations also limit the number of people who can perform their services. The supply is low so the price goes up. If someone discovered the fountain of youth and everyone was healthy, the demand for doctors would go down. But I'd watch out for the person who owns the rights to the fountain. He may have a monopoly and charge you an arm and a leg.

MORALITY AND VALUE

So far we have had no real reason to question whether any part of negotiating (determining the value) had anything to do with morality. A basic transaction is an amoral act—both parties, the buyer and seller, enter into a transaction freely and with their own self-interest in mind. There is nothing right or wrong with it.

We want what we value, and it's what we value that determines the price of something. And if you follow the logic: What we hold as valuable is what we value, and what we value is based upon what we desire, and the final question is, what do we desire?

Now we have moved into the world or morality—the world of our desires. Some desires are very right and some desires are very wrong and others are happily morally neutral—feeding your child is right, killing your child is wrong, and observing your child is morally neutral.

Mac Brown, the head coach of the University of Texas Longhorn football team with a history of championships receives a salary in the millions of dollars. While in contrast, a professor of architecture at the same university may receive a tenth of that, and a local pastor may be paid even less. The perception is that coach Brown is overpaid because he just plays a game while the professor actually teaches students, and the pastor does "God's work."

The question arises, "What is wrong with our values when a football coach get paid 10 times more than a professor or pastor?"

The same question is asked for high school coaches and English or Math teachers whose salaries are not "appropriately" proportioned. Aren't our values backwards when the coach of a game gets paid more than someone who teaches our children—our future? Isn't this a moral problem?

Those who argue that our values are inappropriately placed have a strong point, but when it comes to negotiating, they don't. The issue isn't our morality, the issue is the reality of supply and demand. The problem is that there are too many good teachers and not enough good coaches. If there were a professor who could manage and promote a multi-million dollar football program that pays for itself and other sports, then coach Brown has some competition. And if this were true, the supply doubled (two incredible managers) and the demand stayed the same (one coaching position), so let the negotiations begin and watch the salary fall.

In today's world of values Longhorn football and the University of Texas are so intertwined that they depend on each other. For some strange reason when the football program is winning, the entire university's morale goes up, and interest from both alumni and non-alumni increases—more positive press coverage, better student moral.

If our culture (the general public, the students and professors at the university) had a different value system and athletics were suddenly unpopular, ticket sales would plummet, Coach Brown would be fired and a different coach with a different salary structure would be hired. There is no moral or immoral element to the economics of negotiating, it's just a reflection of our current values—it's our values that are moral or immoral.

Jesus said, "Where your money is, there is your heart also." (Matthew 6: 21) We spend our money on what we value, and this tells us a lot about our modern-day hearts.

A DIFFERENT VIEW OF NEGOTIATIONS

After doing my research, there must be a lot of money to be made through negotiations, because there are myriads of books and expensive seminars produced on the subject. The psychology of buying and selling is a profitable business, and for good reason. Anticipating someone's needs, desires, experiences, family background or even their eating habits in a negotiation can give you the edge when concluding a sale. A "chance" meeting at a local eatery has closed a sale for many a company.

Wise negotiations, as with wisdom in most anything, requires understanding the parties involved as well as the special circumstances surround a negotiation. The more you know the truth about yourself and what you want, the truth about your opponent and what they want, and the more you understand the unique situation involved with the negotiation, the more prepared you will be. And when you add a little creativity or cunning, you will be a shrewd negotiator.

So there you have it. The previous sentence, with a few points on technique and history, is the essence of all the books and seminars on negotiations. They teach you to be shrewd, but seldom do they bring up a very important point— being innocent.

To the modern professor of negotiations, everything is for sale and everything has a price. To them the very key to good negotiations is not to be bound by moral inclinations. It's all about the sale. They've learned to accept a form of philosophy called Moral Relativism—the idea that what is right or wrong is not based on a universal guiding principles, like the character of God, but on our individual preferences (What I feel is right and wrong is not the same as what you feel is right and wrong because we came from different cultures or schools or families).

Gerald Nierenberg, a scholar on the subject, says in his book *The Art of Negotiating*, "We must be careful to realize that our inside world is only a picture of the outside world. We tend to make assumptions about our emotions and thinking. These can confuse us so that we fail to make the distinction between "I feel that..." and "I think that... Assumptions about the extensional world ... can lead us to believe that there are absolutes." Mr. Nierenberg obviously believes there are no absolute guiding principles—that some things are always right and other always wrong.

A friend of mine once quoted a prominent lawyer (to remain nameless), who said, "I'm as honest as time permits." Beware of such shrewd and non-innocent wolves who will say anything to negotiate an extra dollar on a sale, or a piece of your reputation in a lawsuit.

PRICELESS

"Plane tickets to the beach, $500. Two days at a hotel, $300. Plastic tub and shovel, $3. "Watching your son build his first sandcastle: priceless." As the ad says, most things come with a price, but there are some things that are priceless. And for a full view of my point, let me change the wording just a little.

"Plane tickets to the beach, $500. Two days at a hotel, $300. Plastic tub and shovel, $3. "Watching your son come back into consciousness after the paramedics revive him: priceless." I don't mean to be crass, but there are many things that are priceless – some are positive and some negative.

When value is based solely on negotiations, the price is based solely on supply and demand. But there are some things that have high value no matter the negotiating situation.

"What good will it be for a man if he gains the whole world, yet forfeits his soul? Or what can a man give in exchange for his soul?" (Matthew 16:26)

I find it funny how so many of us negotiate with God. "Dear God. If you give me this job, or this girlfriend, or get me out of this jamb, I'll do ..." —as if we could make a deal.

I'm a firm believer in the sovereignty of God and him placing us all in situations to turn us toward him. So it's amusing to me to see all the little negotiations that go on with God over so many years when there is only one thing God wants.

Take the negotiations some go through to please God and get through the pearly gates of heaven. Remember, a real negotiation involves something we want and something someone else wants. And to negotiate well we need to know the truth about ourselves, the other person and the circumstances. I see people negotiating with God, as though there is some cosmic balance weighing their good and bad behavior. They say, "If God sees me doing more good than bad, I'm in!" But my question is, how many goodies covers one big baddy?

In the cosmic balance negotiations, these guys know the truth about themselves—that they fall short of what God wants. They know the truth about all the circumstance in which they fall short. But in the cosmic balance negotiations they make an incorrect assumption about the truths concerning God - what he wants. They think what God wants us to do good things to offset the bad things. What a monotonous and frighteningly insecure game.

Scripture tells us what God wants, and it's completely contrary to the cosmic balance. God wants our whole being—our hearts, minds and bodies. The cosmic balance folks don't accept the concept of Grace (receiving something they don't deserve—gift from God). There is no negotiating with God. You'll lose every time.

"For it is by grace you have been saved, through faith—and this not from yourselves, it is the gift of God—not by works, so that no one can boast. For we are God's workmanship, created in Christ Jesus to do good works, which God prepared in advance for us to do." (Ephesians 2:8—10)

"For Christ died for sins once for all, the righteous for the unrighteous, to bring you to God. He was put to death in the body but made alive by the Spirit." (1 Peter 3:18)

When you get out of negotiating with God and realize there is nothing you have that he wants, when you realize that he loves you like a good father does and was willing to sacrifice for you, and when you release your heart to the things God wants, there is a peace and freedom that overcomes you. It is indescribable to those who haven't experienced it.

It's only after we realize this freedom from negotiations that we can enjoy what living the spiritual life is all about, and how we can fully understand what God wants us to do in our brief time here on earth.

God's grace is priceless. We couldn't pay the price if we had to. So he did. So now we can go about doing what he wants—the pressure is off on this front. Now we can focus on doing the other things our father asks of us—buying, selling, and negotiating in all manner of commerce, being wise, and even shrewd. And we can be innocent, because we know what being right, just and kind is—revealed in the unchanging character of God.

LOVE AND NEGOTIATIONS

Let's say I wanted to sell a plot of land next door to my house and I put it on the market for $100,000. Several prospects come by and look over my property, some saying the land is too expensive and others saying they don't care to live next door to a philosophical author. I get no offers.

Then one day my enemy, someone who wants to kill my family (play along with me here) comes by and says he wants to buy my land. What do I do? I could raise the asking price drastically. In fact, the price couldn't go up high enough for me to sell to this enemy—it's priceless, they couldn't afford it.

Then a day later my mother and father call and say they want to buy it. I love my parents and wouldn't mind them living next door, so I consider lowering the price. I might even consider giving it to them. The price couldn't get any lower than free—it's priceless, there is no price.

So how much is my land actually worth?

The free market doesn't always work—love does tend to

wreak havoc with economic systems. But the question still stands. What would you sell your land for if your enemy or your parents wanted to buy it? What ought a Godly person do?

You should be Godly. We should act like God. And what is God like? He is kind, just and right, and gives grace when it's wise. You should love your neighbor (or your family or friends) as you love yourself.

There is no simple answer to the value of things. In real life there are myriads of factors associated with a single negotiation. But there still is an answer—put the Golden Rule into practice, put yourself in their shoes.

In my case, if my parents wanted to buy the land and I insisted I would give it to them for free, my parents would argue with me for days. They wouldn't see this as fair to me. They love me as I do them, and they want to do what is kind, just and right—as I do.

What a strange argument to be in, "Please let me give this to you!" "No, you spent your hard earned money on that land when you bought it and we don't want you to lose anything by selling it to us!" And without a satisfactory system to make a decision, we would probably go round and round without end.

Years ago I decided to leave a successful partnership with two other architects. They are wonderfully Godly men and good friends. In our deliberations on the value of the business (what was a kind, just and right amount to "buy me out"), we decided to hire an independent third party to determine the value of the company—we would accept whatever this person decided and lovingly go our separate ways. Although I have to admit there were times when some feelings were hurt, the problems were due to miscommunication and improper planning at the beginning of the partnership, not because of distrust in friendships. Eventually we parted ways and have supported and enjoyed each other's friendship ever since. We valued our relationships over the price of the shares in the company.

But just because we loved each other and parted as friends didn't mean the company had no value. Precedents were being set on how to value the company for selling it to future partners or buying it from departing partners, and valuation formulas were being created if the company were to be sold to another entity.

NEGOTIATING FOR THE TEMPLE LAND

King David entered the real estate business when looking for a site to build the temple.

"Then David approached, and when Araunah looked and saw him, he left the threshing floor and bowed down before David with his face to the ground. David said to him, 'Let me have the site of your threshing floor so I can build an altar to the LORD, that the plague on the people may be stopped. Sell it to me at the full price.' Araunah said to David, 'Take it! Let my lord the king do whatever pleases him. Look, I will give the oxen for the burnt offerings, the threshing sledges for the wood, and the wheat for the grain offering. I will give all this.' But King David replied to Araunah, 'No, I insist on paying the full price. I will not take for the LORD what is yours, or sacrifice a burnt offering that costs me nothing. So David paid Araunah six hundred shekels of gold for the site." (2 Samuel 24:21-24)

The heart behind negotiations is to determine value, and sometimes that means finding a price—a kind, just and right price—not to extort or take advantage of your neighbor or business partners.

We live in a world with millions of people who have different wants, needs, values and resources. We don't know that something we value will be valued by someone else, and how much they value it (i.e. what they'll pay for it). If you've been in the business of buying and selling, whether products or services, you've been part of systems for evaluating the price of those products or services. Are they willing to pay $1 or $1 million? Am I willing to sell for $1 or $1 million? You put yourself out in the marketplace and see who bites—the prince or the pauper.

Negotiations, like sales and marketing, is a morally neutral activity. But if we negotiate with a greedy heart or a lust for things to satisfy our worldly desires, then we've crossed over into the world of morality, right and wrong, where the character of God applies, and our integrity is on the line. We should be men and women of integrity, consistently acting the way Godly people should, because we are God's representatives in the business world, and we desire to please and honor God.

13

Competition, Winning and Contentment

"Competition brings out the best in products and the worst in people." David Sarnoff, founder NBC television

"What you are as a person is far more important that what you are as a basketball player." John Wooden, UCLA head basketball coach winning 10 straight national championships in 12 seasons

"Motivation is simple. You eliminate those who are not motivated." Lou Holtz, head football coach at Notre Dame, University of Arkansas, University of South Carolina

"If lessons are learned in defeat, our team is getting a great education." Murray Warmath, football coach at the University of Minnesota

"Yes, it's important that I have good numbers, and I'm well-respected as a player. But I think it's more important that I'm respected as a man." David Robinson, NBA Hall of Fame, philanthropist, founder David Robinson Foundation

COMPETITION

I wish Einstein had been an athlete. If he were, I could refer to him whenever I told someone I competed in college football. Instead, whenever I mention my past athletic experiences I sense my IQ drops 50 points.

At least Plato competed as an athlete. In fact, Plato was not Plato's real name, it was Aristocles. Plato was the name he used when competing as a Greek wrestler, long before he decided to enter the world of philosophy. (I somehow can't see Plato competing on late-night television in the WWF—I think wrestling was a little different back then.) So now I can refer to Plato and keep my IQ up.

Competition occurs everywhere: in football, baseball, and soccer, but it's also an intrinsic part of biology, politics, and economics. We obviously compete in sports, but we also compete for business, we compete for grades or promotions, we may even compete for affection. Competition is everywhere. You can't escape it.

The problem with competition (or the benefit depending on the outcome) is that there is almost always a winner and a loser—it's a problem to the loser, not the winner. Competition can also be very destructive when inappropriately applied.

THE ATHLETIC CONUNDRUM

Back in my high school athletic days, a wise man once asked me a hypothetical question, "If you were in a boxing competition and you knew what your opponent was doing wrong, would you tell him if you knew that by telling him you would lose?"

My immediate answer was, "No way! What idiot would do that?"

He agreed with me briefly, but then pressed the question further, "Why not tell him? You are a Christian aren't you? Aren't you supposed to deny yourself and think of others, show deference to others, your know, the love your neighbor as yourself thing? "

Since I admired this guy I thought about it more and began to feel guilty (religious people are good at guilt, but that wasn't what he was after). He then expanded on his question to a broader view of competition: "What if you were competing against someone trying to kill you? Would you tell him the secret to beating you?" "Of course not," I said.

Then he finally asked, "What if you were playing baseball with your younger brother ... or your son? Would you tell them?"

"Well ... now you're getting into different territory. I don't like my enemy, but I love my brother and would certainly love my son."

"It depends on why you compete, doesn't it," he stated matter of factly. "If you compete against your enemy, you will compete as hard as you can and may try to win at all costs. Why are you competing against your enemy? To survive.

"But in the other case there is a totally different reason to compete—love. When you compete against your brother or son, your desire to teach them how to be better may override your own desire to win—because you love them. You may gladly give up winning to teach your son a lesson."

I hated it when he was right. He won and I lost the philosophical competition. It does depend on why we compete. Knowing why gives meaning to our actions. It reveals guiding principles and tells us what we ought and ought not do.

PROBLEMS WITH COMPETITION

Competition basically involves a relatively simple formula with at least three ingredients. It takes two people and one common prize. If I want the prize and no one else does, when I pursue it I'm not competing with anyone. Or if there are two of us and we want different prizes, we each go on our merry way—there is no competition. Real competition only occurs when there are two or more individuals after the same prize. Boxers compete for a single title, auto manufacturers compete for a buyer, and each warrior competes for a single life—his own.

But sometimes competition can go too far. On January

29, 2009, the girls basketball team of Covenant High School of Dallas beat a lesser opponent with a score of 100 to 0. They were up by 59 points at halftime. Near the end of the game, the winning team's fans grew louder as they reached 100 points, then afterward when the principal and parents demanded an apology from their coach, he said he wouldn't apologize for the wide margin of victory, "When my girls played with honor and integrity." The coach was fired directly.

In the mid 1960s, high school and middle school football coaches were inspired by the words of coach Vince Lombardi, for whom the Super Bowl trophy is named. In the spirit of coach Lombardi's famous statement, "Winning isn't everything, it's the only thing," a generation of impressionable young men, now grown and in business, compete to win at all costs, sacrificing family, money and integrity in the never ending world of competition.

COOPERATION VS. COMPETITION

"I again saw under the sun that the race is not always to the swift, and the battle is not to the warriors, and neither is bread to the wise, nor wealth to the discerning, nor favor to the men of ability ..." (Ecclesiastes 9:11)

Competition is everywhere, but that doesn't mean we should always compete. More times than not, people are after totally different prizes and competition can (and should) be avoided.

John Nash, the subject of the movie "A Beautiful Mind," was a Nobel Prize winning mathematician from Princeton University whose theories on market economics are still used today for artificial intelligence, economics and military theory.

In the movie a scene is set at the local pub where he and his math-nerd friends have gathered to relax and have a drink, when a gorgeous blonde walks into the bar with three attractive girlfriends. As John and his friends discuss the mathematical odds for hooking up with the ladies (math nerds can't help but calculate numerical odds), John has an epiphany.

As he stares at the women, mind racing, he says to his friends, and I'm paraphrasing, "You know, we could all go for the gorgeous blonde, but she will most likely get turned off by everyone pursuing her and not her friends. In that case none of us will have a date tonight. That's the wrong approach.

"Instead we should approach the other three girls first, pleasing the blonde that her friends were included and creating in her a tinge of insecurity. Then when we ask her out also, her fears would be removed and she would be glad to be part of the group. It's a winning scenario for us all."

Dr. Nash's Nobel Prize-winning theories on Governing Dynamics (oversimplified above) revolutionized historic economic theories and changed the process of competition and negotiations for businesses and nations since that time.

In non-sport competitions the variables are usually much more complex than in sport. In boxing, two people are in the ring, playing by the rules to achieve one prize. Only one can win and the other will lose. But in business negotiations, there are many variables and interests and the prizes are not as well defined. Within the simple narrative of the bar scene, there were four men and four women with different motives and different definitions of what the prize was. But they were agreeable to forgo the possibility of a losing competition in order for each friend to have a date.

THREE POSSIBILITIES

There are only three possibilities when two or more individuals, businesses, or nations pursue common prizes. They can all win (commonly known as a win-win scenario), they can all lose (battle to the point that their prizes are no longer worth competing for), or one of them can win and the others lose. Win-win, lose-lose and win-lose—those are the choices.

Win-win is usually the preferable scenario in any business competition. Cooperation, not competition, should be at least considered before diving into the win-lose scenario. Wouldn't we all want to cooperate with others and achieve most of our goals rather than compete with the possibility of achieving none?

Then there is lose-lose. Let's call it the M.A.D. scenario. This was the scenario in which the USA and Russia found themselves during the nuclear arms race from the 1950s until the fall of the USSR in the 1980s. M.A.D. means Mutually Assured Destruction. The USA had thousands of nuclear armed missiles aimed at strategic sites in Russia, and Russia had a similar number pointed at the USA. Each had more missiles than needed to kill the world's population many times over. And because both sides stated that they were ready to use their arsenal, it was certainly maddening. M.A.D.-ness kept the world at peace during the times known as the Cold War.

But as technology advanced and the US began experimenting with armed satellites to defend our country, the balance of power shifted—an imbalance that created concerns on the Russian side. So Ronald Reagan, the president at this time, stated that if the USA's technological superiority created a greater chance for nuclear war, we would simply give the technology to Russia in order to maintain the balance, continuing the M.A.D. but peaceful scenario.

So there are the win-win and the lose-lose/M.A.D. scenarios. But if you think about it, the lose-lose and the win-win scenarios are actually not competition at all. The are mutual cooperation—maybe forced cooperation, but cooperation none the less.

True competition only exists when there is the real possibility of a winner and loser. Only when the balance of power is broken does real competition begin.

WHY WE COMPETE

As discussed at the beginning of the book, if we know why we do something, we discover guiding principles. Answers to the questions who, what, when, where and how only tell what is, while why is the only question that delivers moral imperatives—what we ought and ought not do. Who we compete against, what we compete for, when we compete for it, and where the competition takes place only provide a bunch of facts about the competition. It's the why we compete—the desire, the motivation behind our competitive acts—that moves competition into the world of morality.

For example, when I compete with a technology company for a big project, if I break into their offices, grab their trade secrets to use them for my benefit, I have not only broken the law, I have acted immorally. However, if I break into their offices and grab their trade secrets, not to use in competition but to keep them from being destroyed in a fire, I have acted morally. My actions were exactly the same. It's my motives and desires that tip the scale from what's immoral to moral.

In my experience, I believe we compete for three reasons: We compete to win, we compete to grow, and we compete for show. Depending on the type competition, depending on your personality, your gifts, or the person or company you compete with, you will compete for one, two or all three of these reasons—to win, to grow, or for show.

Now after reading this, my friends, the serious entrepreneurs and athletes out there, will leap up and insist, "Why compete except to win? What is this grow and show nonsense?"

Believe me, I know these guys. Competition is what drives them. There is always another competition out there—another mountain to climb, business to start, or extreme sport to try. It's almost an addiction to competition, the desire to win "gone wild." It's the thrill of the hunt, not the prize that drives them. To these guys the win is satisfying—but only for a short while—until the next competition entices them with another possibility to win.

In one of his letters, Paul gives Timothy some advice about winning and competition. He refers to the antithesis of this desire for another win—contentment.

"But godliness with contentment is great gain... But if we have food and clothing, we will be content with that. People who want to get rich fall into temptation and a trap and into many foolish and harmful desires ..." (1 Timothy 6: 6-9)

Paul also told the Philippian church, "I know what it is to be in need, and I know what it is to have plenty. I have learned the secret of being content in any and every situation, whether well fed or hungry, whether living in plenty or in want." (Philippians 4:12)

Contentment is the opposite of the fleeting desire for one more win. It is the calm assurance that God has things under control, and given us everything we need for the moment.

Again, I can see my competitive friends squirm in their seats and ask, "Well, you know, this sounds all nice and peaceful, but I still have a question as an athlete and businessman. Does this mean I shouldn't compete at all, much less compete to win? Should I just sit around all content-like, happily watching the grass grow and never compete again?"

I don't think that's what Paul meant, because he also said, "... Run is such a way that you may win." (1 Corinthians 9:24). And he said, "I press on toward the goal to win the prize for which God has called me ..." (Philippians 3:14)

Competition is a good thing when appropriately applied. It is a tool to be used for reasons other than fulfilling the endless desire to attain another win.

TO GROW

Others see competition as a tool to grow their wealth or influence. They would say, "We live in a Darwinian world and only the strong survive at sport, business or anything else." Live strong or die hard. Their desire is to literally grow to a point that there are no longer any competitors. They don't want to weaken competition, they want to eliminate the it—horde it all, compete to the exclusion of everyone. They covet—the very definition of greed.

George Reisman, professor of economics at Pepperdine University, would say to them, "Whoever claims that economic competition represents 'survival of the fittest' in the sense of the law of the jungle, provides the clearest possible evidence of their lack of knowledge of economics." Competition as a tool for growth shouldn't eliminate competition, it should foster more of it and provide motivation for advancement in life, business and athletics. We should all grow because of it—spiritually, economically, athletically, whatever.

The construction field is very competitive. There are winners and losers every day. When my company receives an opportunity to bid on a project, we compete hard, we know our strengths and weaknesses, we know our competitor's strengths and weaknesses, we know what it costs for us to do business, and we know how much profit we wish to make to cover unforeseen risks. The whole of the activity of competition makes us grow as a company. We don't necessarily grow in size. We grow in efficiency and often character.

When my daughters were in high school, our sport of choice was volleyball. Wise counsel led my wife and I to believe that having our girls compete in a team sport would benefit their character as young women. Trust me on this, keeping teenagers tired, busy and pursuing a common goal is a very good thing. Having them work under the leadership of a strict coach (which is hard for some, easy for others), and having them compete alongside girls with different talents, faiths, and family baggage, offers great opportunities for growth and maturity. My business, my employees, my girls (now women) all grew better using the tool of competition.

Paul knew this, "...Everyone who competes in the games exercises self-control in all things ... I buffet my body and make it my slave, lest possibly, after I have preached to others, I myself should be disqualified." (1 Corinthians 9:24-27)

Paul was content in who he was, but he was not content with what or where he was as a person growing in maturity. He was a secure child of God. That's what made him content. He was content with living in both hunger and plenty, because of who God has made him, not because of his situations. I'm pretty sure Paul would have preferred having food when he was hungry, but food didn't affect him because he knew who he was and what he was put on this earth to do. On the other hand, Paul was not content with what or where he was in his growth as a God-loving person. There are always struggles and the need to grow.

FOR SHOW

Finally there is competing for show, to show off your talents—the desire for status, significance or reputation.

Having competed in the higher levels of sport I've observed some amazing talents—young men who barely had any competition, but yet they still competed. LeBron James became one of the most celebrated rookies in NBA history coming directly out of high school. But he still competed in high school even though he knew he could defeat anyone who challenged him. He competed to "show" the fans and scouts that he was the best—and worthy of the big bucks.

Looking back, I think Mohamed Ali, Michael Jordon, and Earl Campbell could claim the same thing. When it came to size, speed and agility, these were men playing among boys.

Their talents were gifts. They didn't work to get there, God made them that way.

And as they became more aware (most likely as teenagers) that they were becoming larger and faster than their peers they were faced with a question and a choice. It was one of their first existential questions—why they existed that way. And they had to answer the question one of two ways. They could answer, "I am special because I made myself this way (and I deserve it)," or they could say, "I am special because of someone else (and I am humbled and appreciative of it)?"

Unfortunately, many gifted athletes chose to think they were special because they deserve it. And as they move up the ladder of success from high school to college and to the pros, they become more and more self absorbed.

These guys didn't compete to win or to grow in high school. Winning came too easy for them—why go through the trouble to exert yourself if the competition is that easy? Yet, they still competed. They didn't compete to grow. They competed to show-off their abilities.

Fortunately, there was another group who made another choice. As they became aware of their talents and realized they were gifts, these guys were humbled and thankful for the opportunity to win. They accepted praise with difficulty. After scoring a touchdown, instead of pumping their fists in the air, they followed their hearts and ran back and celebrated with the team of linemen who got him there. After a slam dunk the first thing that came to mind was the pass that got them the ball. Or when a job is awarded, the first thing that comes to the boss' mind (and out of his mouth) is his appreciation for the team that worked so hard to win.

All these guys compete for show, but with a different heart and motive.

BALANCE OR PEACEFUL TENSION

When we compete in athletics or business, we often times compete with all three desires—to win, to grow and to show off who you are. All have there positives and negatives, but we use them all.

But sometimes these three motivations actually compete against each other, and we grapple with our consciences on which is the right or wrong way to complete. What's more important, winning the prize, growing as a company, or competing to show off who we are and how well we can do business?

So how do we deal with competing motivations? How do we keep them in balance?

After reading many books in the attempt to balance my life, and after wrestling with my conscience and observing life over my many years, I've come to believe it is impossible to achieve a balanced life. If I only had two things to deal with I could possibly pull it off. But my life is more of a juggling act than a balancing act, with balls, bowling pins, chainsaws and flaming torches all tossed in the air at the same time. My life would be better described as the constant tension of keeping everything in the air—focusing on the important things while the less important things still flash in front of my view.

However, although I don't believe balance is truly possible, I do believe you can have peace within the tension created by juggling the things around you. Balance is illusive, but there can be peaceful tension.

To have peace while juggling, first and possibly foremost you should have confidence in your juggling skills. You should be good at it before you throw too many things in the air. Even a skilled juggler can track only a few items at a time. But when you know your juggling skills and have an appropriate number of things in the air, you can actually juggle in peace.

But sometimes, and through no fault of you own, a stray bowling ball gets thrown into your peaceful juggling act, and you realize one item will have to drop or they may all come tumbling down.

The wise juggler of life's events has already considered the possibility of one falling and knows which item has priority. He knows which one can fall and which one must be kept up at all costs. The juggler who knows why he or she is here and the guiding principles in their lives can find peace in the midst of the difficult circumstances. Do I answer my wife's cell during a business meetings? Do you compete honestly even though you know everyone else is breaking the rules? When a hurting friend is late for a meeting, pushing your schedule by an hour, do you cancel your next business meeting or blow off your friend? Knowing your priorities is the only way to peaceful juggling.

Jesus was in the middle of a rather tense time the days before his crucifixion. But his thoughts, his priorities, were on his disciples, not himself. He knew he was going to die an agonizing death and accepted that fact, but he was concerned that his followers wouldn't understand. With all the things he had going on in his life, he said, "Peace I live to you: my peace I give to you. I do not give to you as the world gives."

Balance is next to impossible for busy people, but we can have peace in tension when our priorities are as they should be.

REVERSED PRIORITIES

So if there are three reasons for competing (to win, to grow and for show), which one should have priority?

As mentioned at the beginning of this chapter, cooperation is usually best tried first—cooperation, not competition. Your potential competitor may have a different desire than you—a different prize in mind. Why compete when you can both win?

But when those who's desire is to please and honor God actually compete, scripture guides them to the priority list. We should first compete to show, then to grow and lastly to win. Let me explain.

In one of his first public talks, the Sermon on the Mount, Jesus told his disciples, "You are the light of the world. A city on a hill cannot be hidden. Neither do people light a lamp and put it under a bowl. Instead they put it on its stand, and it gives light to everyone in the house. In the same way, let your light shine before men, that they may see your good deeds and praise your Father in heaven. (Matthew 5:14—16)

With the same idea in mind Paul tells the Corinthian church, "We are therefore Christ's ambassadors, as though God were making his appeal through us." (2 Corinthians 5:20)

If our desire is to please and honor God, whether we like it or not, we represent God and his character, just as an ambassador represents his king and country. When someone knows you claim to be a follower of Christ, you have unintentionally volunteered to show them what God is like—in all areas of your life—sports, family, business, everywhere.

I recall a talk my former coach Darrell Royal had with the entire team regarding one student athlete making a fool of himself (as many college football players tend to do). "Do you think the press cares that it was you, Jim Bob, who pulled that stupid stunt? No. They don't write about Jim Bob. Instead they write, 'Texas Longhorn Football Player' pulled the stunt and they don't mention your name at all. Your actions reflect on our entire team."

When we represent the entire world of Godliness, we should show what God is like before considering growing or winning.

Eric Liddell was fast, and he knew it. At one time he was the fastest man in the world, winning gold in the Olympic Games in 1924. But he was also humbled by his wealth of talent—his gift. He grew up in China, the son of Scottish missionaries whose view of the Sabbath was more rigid than many of us hold today. But he was strong in his belief that the Sabbath was holy and he determined in his heart not to compete on Sunday. When the schedule for the Olympic races was issued and he found one of his races was to be run on Sunday, he chose not to run—against the urging of his coaches and country's leaders. And because of his convictions and his choice to please God instead of himself or others, the word spread about the runner who would give up Olympic gold for his faith.

Eric did win gold, but in a different race held on a different day. He was quoted as saying, "I believe God made me for a purpose, but he also made me fast. And when I run, I feel His pleasure." Eric knew his priorities and competed to show who he was first, and after that, he competed to win. And he inspired millions of God loving athletes who came after him.

"Therefore, since we have so great a cloud of witnesses surrounding us (people observing our show), let us lay aside every encumbrance, and the sin which so easily entangles us, and let us run with endurance the race set before us." (Hebrews 12:1)

Paul says, "...I run in such a way, as not without aim ... lest possibly, after I have preached (showing myself) to others, I myself should be disqualified." (1 Corinthians 9:26—27)

TO GROW

Our next priority is to grow—both the growth of ourselves and others. Winning is great and losing is disappointing, but both can be useful for growth. Growth and maturity are more important than winning, and God is more concerned with who you are than what you do.

"Everyone who competes in the games exercises self-control in all things... Therefore I run in such a way, as not without aim; I box in such a way, as not beating the air; but I discipline my body and make it my slave..." (1 Corinthians 9:25-26)

Sometimes we win and God grows us, but sometimes we lose badly (in competition and often times morally) and God teaches us some hard truths.

"...My son, do not make light of the Lord's discipline, and do not lose heart when he rebukes you, because the Lord disciplines those he loves, and he punishes everyone he accepts as a son. Endure hardship as discipline; God is treating you as sons... No discipline seems pleasant at the time, but painful. Later on, however, it produces a harvest of righteousness and peace for those who have been trained by it. Therefore, strengthen your feeble arms and weak knees. Make level paths for your feet, so that the lame may not be disabled, but rather healed. Make every effort to live in peace with all men and to be holy; without holiness no one will see the Lord." (Hebrews 12:4-17)

TO WIN

Well, all this sounds nice and spiritual, doesn't it? But, what about winning? Should we just sit around, meditating on how we can best show ourselves as being Godly ambassadors, hoping we grow into passive men and women?

Wrong! Competition is hard and fun and exceptionally useful! We should strategize, plan, implement and compete hard—to win! And while doing so, we show our competitors and spectators who we are—people who desire to please and honor God.

"Do you not know that those who run in a race all run, but only one receives the prize? Run in such a way that you may WIN. Everyone who competes in the games exercises self-control in all things. They then do it to receive a perishable wreath, but we an imperishable." (1 Corinthians 9:24)

Of course we compete to win, but we compete for different reasons. The "world" competes for things that will satisfy temporarily—championship rings, more clients, more money, or the celebrity that goes with it all. But we compete for a prize that won't go away. And as we'll see in the next chapters, the prize we compte for is fulfilling and eternal.

14

Risk, Insurance and Faith

"You've got to go out on a limb sometimes because that's where the fruit is." Will Rogers, American humorist, social commentator

"The greatest danger of insurance is that it easily undermines our dependence on God. I must carefully evaluate my motives when it comes to buying insurance. Is it a God-given means of provision? Or is it an end-run that makes trust obsolete and God unnecessary?" Randy Alcorn, Money Possessions and Eternity

"Confidence doesn't come out of nowhere. It's a result of something... hours and days and weeks and years of constant work and dedication." Roger Staubach, Heisman Trophy winner at Naval Academy, quarterback Dallas Cowboys, founder Staubach Company, real estate investment firm

"Faith is a living and unshakable confidence, a belief in the grace of God so assured that a man would die a thousand deaths for its sake." Martin Luther, 15th century German priest and founder of the Protestant Reformation

RISKY BUSINESS

"Winning the lottery isn't always what it's cracked up to be," said Evelyn Adams who won the New Jersey lottery not just once, but twice (in 1985 and 1986), to the tune of $5.4 million. Today the money is all gone and Adams lives in a trailer. "Everybody wanted my money. Everybody had their hand out. I never learned one simple word in the English language—'No.' I wish I had the chance to do it all over again. I'd be much smarter about it now."

Evelyn Adams risked a few dollars and reaped millions. Then she risked the millions and reaped some hard life's lessons.

Risk. It's everywhere. When you get into your car to drive to work, the odds of you dying in a wreck are 1 in 247. However, if you ride the bus to work they're only 1 in 94,242. Risky business isn't it—just waking up and going to work every morning.

Your chances of dying from a lightning strike are 1 in 80,000, from a snake attack 1 in 250,000. When you wake up in the morning and walk to the bathroom, where most fatal home accidents occur each year, you are gambling with your life? Gambling, Wagering, Risk. It's as prevalent as competition.

I've never purchased a Lotto ticket (a decision I made when the system was first made legal), but I gamble everyday. There's only a 1 in 200 million chance of buying the winning the Powerball Lotto ticket. With those odds, I might as well throw my money in the air and see if other bills join them as they fall back neatly into my wallet. Risk is something you can't escape. We weigh and balance risks with each decision we make everyday, many times without being fully conscious of it.

Say you purchase a piece of chocolate, open the wrapper and throw it into your mouth. But as it passes (in slow motion) in front of your eyes and onto your tongue, you notice a small white spot on the brown confection. In milliseconds your brain begins the process of risk assessment. Was that white spot a stain, a patch of fungus? A bug? Depending on the "certainty analysis system" lying somewhere between your temporal lobe and the sick feeling in the pit of your stomach, you either begin chewing or—"yuk!" You spit it out.

Risk is a given, yes, but the question I have related to business and Godliness is this: "What risk ought we or ought we not be involved in?" Is there a moral element to risk?

RISK, GAMBLING AND MORALITY

Risk by itself is just a measurement of mathematical odds. Saying risk is either right or wrong is like saying the number 2 is right and the number 3 is wrong. Risk is not the issue. Like any issue with morality it's the desire behind the risk that makes it right or wrong. Just because something is low risk doesn't make it right and we have permission to do it, and just because something is high risk doesn't mean we avoid it. The risks of you're child being involved in an auto accident are relatively low, but you buckle them up anyway—and not just because it is the law. The risks involved in climbing into a burning car to save your child are very high, but you'd do it in a second.

Dealing with the world of risk involves dealing with the unknowns, the uncertainties of life—very similar to faith. Will a drunk driver swerve in front of your car? We simply don't know. Yet we still get into our cars and drive to work because we have a certain element of faith in the traffic system and the hundreds of drivers we pass on the road.

But let's take risk and faith a step further into the world of gambling. Let's be honest. Their is a fine line between risk and gambling. If you are an investor, you buy (invest in) stocks and bonds because you are risking your money that the market price will increase over time, and you sell (divest from) them just as quickly when you think the market price will drop. Before investing, you do our research (or trust those who say they have done the research), find the odds are reasonable enough, and you exchange your money for the stock.

Take your work. When you go to work for a particular company, you have invested in that company, whether you like it or not. By risking your education, experience and time in exchange for salary, benefits and a job you're waging your financial life that the business owners were wise, that the economy is strong, and that the business will actually stay in business. If one of these factors changes (the economy slows or the owners decide to buy toxic assets) you will be out on your own, looking for a different job. Or on the positive side (I am actually an optimist), if factors change and the owners are wise, and you and your fellow employees work efficiently, your salary, benefits and job security go up.

Your safety, your money and your job are all susceptible to a vast degree or risk every day of every year. And with that risk come degrees of faith in your company, your boss, your fellow workers—and possibly the God "who works all things together for the good of those who love him..." (Romans 8:28). There is a direct correlation between risk and faith.

LOW, MODERATE AND HIGH RISK

Let's analyze risk by separating it into three categories: low, moderate, and high—walking out the door on a normal clear day (low risk), walking out the door in the rain (moderate risk), and walking out the door in a flood (high risk). Or another way of looking at it—telling your boss, Good morning! Hey, good lookin! or Get lost!

Most of us would say it takes very little faith and do something in the low risk category. We equate low risk with a low faith requirement. And when uncertainties grow in our minds, the risk level grows higher as well, and our faith requirement must increase. Low risk takes little or no faith, moderate risk takes moderate faith, and extremely high risk takes outright blind faith (Go ahead and buy that stock in the Afghan startup company from an internet site that said they would give you 100% return on your investment). The lower the risk the less the faith, the higher the risk the more the faith it takes to act. Right?

Believe it or not, that's entirely backward. Faith, real bibli-cal faith, is a measure of certainty not uncertainty. Faith is mental evidence—a deep down in your heart conviction. It is that thing that gives you the motivational kick in the pants to risk your money, your job or your life. If you think faith is just something we muster up in the hope that the worst won't happen, then you have the concept of faith in reverse.

The writer of Hebrews defined biblical faith.

"Faith is the evidence of things hoped for, the conviction of things not seen." (Hebrews 11:1)

If faith was built around uncertainty (rather than cer-tainty) when you told a friend, "I have faith in you," you've just insulted them. You've just told them you have little con-fidence, but hope everything works out in spite of them. This is backwards. When you tell someone you have faith in them, you are paying them a compliment. You are telling them you have confidence in them.

Biblical faith is confidence and assurance—an internal unseen, convinced-in-your-mind, deep-in-your-heart evi-dence. It's a confidence and assurance that tells you it is right to take action because you know it's the right thing to do. Real faith is jumping out of the airplane with a good and tested parachute, not jumping out in the hope that someone put a chute in your pack. At the moment of deci-sion to jump, you either jump or you don't because of that faith—it's like an on/off switch.

Faith should be conviction so strong it would be an af-front to God not to do what your faith was leading you to do.

REAL FAITH

When Abraham (Abram at the time) made up his mind to move from his homeland and launch his family toward an unknown country, do you think he packed and moved because he was uncertain? No. Abraham trusted God, and that faith and trust was certain enough for him to pack up everything and move.

When Daniel's friends, Shadrach, Meshach and Abednego, were about to be thrown into the fire for intentionally neglecting an edict of King Nebuchadnezzar, were they timid about their decision? No. They said to the king, "...We do not need to defend ourselves before you in this matter. If we are thrown into the blazing furnace, the God we serve is able to save us from it, and he will rescue us from your hand, O king. But even if he does not, we want you to know, O king, that we will not serve your gods or worship the image of gold you have set up." (Daniel 3: 16-18)

Without a gift of faith, I don't think they could have done this. It would take supernatural faith (something only God could give) for me to even consider doing what these three young men did. Their faith was strong enough—meaning their convictions were deep enough—that they made the choice. Baring a miracle they chose to burn in a furnace rather than go against their promises to God. They believed God would save them, but even if he didn't, they were going into the furnace because it was the right thing to do.

Did this little beginning of a sentence, "But even if he does not," show a lack of faith? No. Their faith was in what they knew, not in what they did not know. They knew the promises they had made and they hoped to avoid burning. But they acted on what they knew—an inner evidence of what their convictions were—faith.

The risk formula should read opposite from what we normally think. The more you know about the risks on your safety, money, or family, the more faith, certainly, and confidence you have of the outcome. The less you know of the risks, the less faith you act upon—to the point of foolishness.

RISKS AND TESTING GOD

When Jesus was fasting and taken to a mountain in the wilderness, one of the temptations Satan threw at him was: "If you are the Son of God, throw yourself down. For it is written: 'He will command his angels concerning you, and they will lift you up in their hands, so that you will not strike your foot against a stone.' Jesus answered him, 'It is also written: 'Do not put the Lord your God to the test.'" (Matthew 4: 6-7)

Risk and faith go hand in hand, but some risky behaviors are so foolish they could be called sinful. Putting yourself on the edge of a cliff and telling onlookers, "Will you believe in God if I jump off and God saves me?" is not a good idea. It's not faith—that's putting God to the test.

In the same way, it's not a faithful prayer for a job interview when you say, "God, I have no education, no talent nor any experience in this field of work. Please let them hire me." If you were hired, I would call it a miracle of God's grace, but not an act of faith. The wise and faithful way to go into the job market is with a good education, valuable experiences, research on the companies you wish to work for, and a prayer that God will give you insight into his will for your choices.

I know there is always an element of doubt and uncertainty in any risky venture, from stepping into your car to changing jobs, but when you act in faith you act with certainty, and it outweighs the risk.

Faith is that certainty you sense before making a hard decision. It is a deep inner confidence in the things you know, a confidence that overshadows the uncertainties that are there. I believe this faith is a gift from God—starting with scripture's leading, then good and Godly counsel, from the use of our God given mental faculties, and then finally (subsequently) from prayerful, inner peace and confidence that drives you to take action.

Even though there are still instances where God's calling

may appear outlandish and the risks are very high, it is still our confidence in God that leads us to do something for him. When we act in great confidence and peace, we are revealing our faith. When we act in great uncertainty, we don't.

DEALING WITH RISK

But now, back to the practical world. How do we deal with the risks in our lives—low, moderate and high risks?

We act wisely and insure against risks where we can.

I'm not saying that the conclusion to this whole philosophical discussion about risk and faith is to buy, of all things, insurance. The conclusion is to gain practical assurance (confidence) against the various types of risks you come across.

When you understand the possibility of being thrown out of your car, what do you do to cover that risk? You simply buckle your seat belt. When you are worried that you may be over your head in purchasing a new house (concerned about the financial risks to you and your family), what do you do? You seek the guidance of someone who has been there before, someone who has successfully navigated through the waters of mortgages and family expenses. When you are curious whether to pursue a different job offer, you are wise to find assurance before putting on your parachute and jumping out of the company plane.

Wise and Godly counsel will take you to scripture for examples and principles that will guide your decisions. They will take you through their experiences and offer advice on pitfalls or opportunities you may have never considered.

WHAT IF

The risks you encounter obviously guide the type of assurance you need. Physical safety risks involve physical safety assurance. Future employment risks involve future employment assurance. And financial risks involve financial assurance.

So, how do you assess these risks and what do you do to gain the faith and confidence you need to be wise?

One thing you can do is play a game called "What if?"

"What if I don't buckle my child up in their safety seat?" You run the risk of getting a ticket, but more importantly you run the risk of death.

"What if the stock market tanks?"

"What if my boss breaks the law?"

"What if my house burns down?"

What if ... what if ... what if?

There are what if questions about safety that are answered by changing your behavior—like wearing a seat belt. But then there are the what if questions about other things, like the money to pay the medical bills of the person you injured in an auto accident. And these questions lead you to purchase insurance. Financial risks should be covered by a financial assurance.

"What if I die before I'm 30?"

Are you married? Does your wife have a good paying job? Do you have children? If so, would your dying put your family in bad financial straits? Probably so. But if you are not married with children, you may not need to purchase an life insurance policy.

What if your apartment or house burned down? Is the investment you have in furniture, clothing, and artwork at risk of burning away? Do you have enough money to buy all that stuff again? Or is it worth a monthly payment to transfer that risk onto a company that has resources (a pool of thousands of people like you) who will pay you in case it all goes up in smoke?

Insurance companies are just good risk takers—very scientific, but good risk takers. Like the odds makers in Las Vegas, they know the odds and cover the spreads. Their scientists, called actuaries, have calculated the risk of everything imaginable—the odds of someone just like you dying from a bath tub fall or sky diving accident. I actually met an actuary once and was surprised that he looked and acted like a normal person. But I knew back in his office he had five computers reading the latest medical findings on the cancer risk in Skandanavian furniture polish and its relation to the life expectancy of Hispanic Americans living near the Rio Grande River in southern Texas. They have all the data on a mile-wide spreadsheet and they're the guys that set the price of your insurance coverage.

LIVING WISELY

But buying insurance is not the answer to every risk. What if I retire and Social Security isn't there to help me pay for the house, my medical bills, or my life?

"In the house of the wise are stores of choice food and oil, but the foolish man devours all he has." (Proverbs 21:20)

"Go to the ant, you sluggard; consider its ways and be wise! It has no commander, no overseer or ruler, yet it stores its provisions in summer and gathers its food at harvest." (Proverbs 6:6-8)

Joseph, through the inspiration of God, created a plan to save food for a coming famine which decimated Egypt for seven years.

It is very wise to work and save to lower the risks of retirement, and these are just a few examples of the counsel you can find in scripture. But wise and frugal living will not always save us from the risks of life. Jesus adds this story.

"The ground of a certain rich man produced a good crop. He thought to himself, 'What shall I do? I have no place to store my crops.' Then he said, 'This is what I'll do. I will tear down my barns and build bigger ones, and there I will store all my grain and my goods. And I'll say to myself, You have plenty of good things laid up for many years. Take life easy; eat, drink and be merry.' But God said to him, 'You fool! This very night your life will be demanded from you. Then who will get what you have prepared for yourself?' This is how it will be with anyone who stores up things for himself but is not rich toward God." (Luke 20:16-21)

Through all this practical discussion regarding risk, we should never forget why we are here and that life is not short, but eternal. We are here to please and honor God by loving him and our neighbors, earnestly seeking to know and do what God wants, for ourselves and those we are responsible for.

As much as I believe in wise and Godly counsel, I equally believe that those who love God, those who strongly desire to please and honor Him, have a spiritual connection—a sixth sense, a still quite inaudible inner voice, a heart for what is right and true. And it's this connection that guides us past the "what ifs" of moving forward in Godliness. It is a peace from God that surpasses understanding.

What if I die?

When my body lies decaying, what happens to the "breath of life" that lives on? What happens to me, my soul, my spirit? Does it simply vanish into the void? Am I absorbed into the cosmic universe, transformed into another form of life? Or am I suddenly in the presence of God. May I recommend you find assurance in this area of risk? It will affect the decisions you make for the rest of your life.

15

Debt, Lending and Patience

"A banker is a fellow who lends you his umbrella when the sun is shining, but wants it back the minute it begins to rain." Mark Twain, aka Samuel L. Clemens, 19th century writer and humorist

"Debt is the slavery of the free" Publilius Synus, Roman author, 1st century B.C.

"If I owe you a pound, I have a problem; but if I owe you a million, the problem is yours." John Keynes, 20th century English economist, journalist, and financier

"Christmas is the season when you buy this year's gifts with next year's money." Anonymous (avid shopper)

"Do not be a man who strikes hands in pledge or puts up security for debts; if you lack the means to pay, your very bed will be snatched from under you." (Proverbs 22:26-27) Solomon, King of Israel 10th century B.C., writer of Ecclesiastes and most of Proverbs.

YOU OWE ME

As long as there have been neighbors, there's been a neighbor who needed to borrow something. It's very possible that some nomad loaned his camel to a friend, who promptly mistreated it and returned it a month later without an oat-bag fill up. Little has changed when it comes to relationships between people. Borrowing and lending has had its pitfalls from the first neighbor to the current universe of international credit and monetary policy.

The earliest lending system grew from the cyclical nature of agriculture and merchant trade. In the off times, between planting and harvesting their crops, farmers needed money to live and maintain the farms. Merchants on the other hand needed money to buy items they would resell much later. So each would borrow money from someone with means, usually the king, who quite literally had a vested interest in the economy. (Can anyone say taxes?)

Around 1750 B.C. the Babylonian kingdom at the height of its influence, began to write rules to stabilize lending, which in turn encouraged even more of it (and, by the way, consolidated more power in the hands of the king—politicians haven't changed much). The Hummurabi Code was written outlining limits on interest that could be charged —a maximum of 33% on farm loans and 20% on money lending—and the time required to pay back the loans. Later interest rates began to drop and eventually settled between 6% and 12%.

Lending in ancient times was a simple one-on-one transaction—someone (the king, a friend, or a relative) had $1,000 in his possession and loaned out $1,000. The borrower in turn paid back $1,000 with interest or a fee (if required).

Modern banking and lending is quite a different thing, starting with the goldsmiths of England who gave out paper receipts to those who deposited gold into their banks. After an imaginative goldsmith (who noticed that seldom did any of their depositors come back and get all their gold) began giving out more paper receipts (or banknotes) than he actually had in gold in his bank—lending more money than they had on deposit.

This morally questionable practice gained in popularity and spread to Europe. No wonder John Calvin declared that professional moneylenders should be banned from the church. And Martin Luther said, "After the devil there is no greater human enemy on earth than a miser and usurer (referring to bankers), for he desires to be above everyone."

But then an interesting thing happened. These bankers and their friends in government found that the more banknotes were floating around, the more things people could buy, creating a demand for more things to be created, and the economy grew. As long as no one noticed that the banknotes they used weren't backed by anything, everything ran just fine. But the problem was, when there were signs of economic trouble and everyone ran back to the bank to exchange their paper banknotes for their gold (the dreaded run on the bank), there wasn't enough gold to give back.

Nowadays, we've legalized this system of over lending, but in our sophisticated modern way we have a much more complex system of over lending. It's called Fractional Reserve Banking with myriads of rules and regulations too numerous to state here, all backed by the good faith and credit of our government.

It's a little scary isn't it? But that's ok. We've been doing it for around 100 years and we're still here. And if our government fell apart, who would want our dollars anyway? So as long as our money, leveraged through fractional reserve banking, keeps expanding and contracting exponentially with economic cycles (like the long end of a unbalanced "see-saw") and our money is backed by our faith in government, we are happy to keep on buying and selling with our dollars.

PROBLEMS WITH DEBT

There are many good and Godly people who believe that going into debt of any kind is against the wise counsel of scripture. They justify their positions by quoting verses such as:

"The rich rule over the poor, and the borrower is servant to the lender." (Proverbs 22:7), or "Let no debt remain outstanding." (Romans 13:8), or "Do not be a man who strikes hands in pledge or puts up security for debts; if you lack the means to pay, your very bed will be snatched from under you." (Proverbs 22:26-27)

Not a pretty picture. But these verses don't actually state that the world of debt is immoral or wrong. They only state the fact that debt strains relationships and the one in debt is actually in a risky spot—in debt to the lender. He must pay back the loan or else he may lose his bed or become a bond servant to the lender (a common practice in biblical times). The more debt the less freedom you have to sleep, work or play.

But the Bible actually doesn't discouraged debt and lending. In fact lending was encouraged with recommendations on how a Godly person should do it. There were loans for business and loans for compassion, and those who followed God's teaching knew the difference.

Access to money was very scarce in biblical times and loaning to a family member or neighbor in financial straights was very different than loaning money to a foreigner who was going to make a profit with the use of your money. Very little is mentioned in scripture about lending for business purposes, but that doesn't mean it wasn't commonplace. Lenders for business would charge either a one time fee or interest over time. The only thing the Godly lender was expected do, according to scripture, was to not take advantage of the borrower. A lender should charge a reasonable rate or fee in relation to the risk involved in the loan and not take advantage of someone in need of basic necessities.

"He who increases his wealth by exorbitant interest amasses it for another, who will be kind to the poor." (Proverbs 28:8)

You might ask, as I did, what then is a reasonable fee or interest rate for the risk? Unfortunately there is no principle in scripture outlining good or bad interest rates, but it does speak of Usury. Usury (an unusually high or burdensome interest rate) is frowned upon. But what is usury? I don't think we can define it here, but somehow I think the parties involved in a loan knew what it was when they negotiate terms.

There are those who would define usury as charging even the slightest bit of interest, and when loaning money to your family or neighbors, it should be without interest. But we live in different economic times. Since the modern monetary system typically has inflation built into it, if someone made a loan with no interest and the borrower paid it back over several years, the lender would actually receive less money as the years went by due to inflation.

The Bible is pretty specific about certain kinds of lending—within the immediate family and within the family of God. When it comes to loaning to a family member, or someone in legitimate need, the Godly thing to do is to make a loan and charge no interest at all.

"Do not charge your brother interest, whether on money or food or anything else that may earn interest. (Deuteronomy 23:19)

"Rather be openhanded and freely lend him whatever he needs." (Deuteronomy 15:8)

But even in light of this, God doesn't expect everyone to refrain from charging interest for all occasions. Jesus referred to the charging of interest as a normal part of doing business when telling his parable of the talents.

"Well then, you should have put my money on deposit with the bankers, so that when I returned I would have received it back with interest." (Matthew 25:27)

Scripture advises us when lending money, that we should be compassionate with our family and friends in need (not even expecting repayment in some circumstances), but when financing commercial activity, which involves a different measure of risk and the expectation of profit, charging interest is not frowned upon.

DEBT OR PARTNERSHIP

Let's look at lending and debt a little deeper, because when you begin to analyze it, you'll find that not all loans should be considered debt.

Do you have a mortgage on your home or a loan on your car? If so, have you read the entire loan agreement? You may be surprised that your mortgage may not be considered debt at all. It is more of a partnership.

A typical loan agreement for a house will read roughly something like this: You agree to buy a house for "x" dollars so the lender loans you the money. You promise to pay back the loan with monthly payments of "y". Since it says "you promise to pay" the money back, the average person would think you have done something unethical or immoral if you stop paying back the loan.

However, if you read the rest of the loan agreement, there is another clause: However, if you fail to make payments of "y," we the lender have the right to take back the house and sell it to get our money back, and then the debt will be considered paid.

This isn't a debt so much as it is a partnership. The lender and the person receiving the loan entering an agreement with a planned way out. No wonder John Keynes, the old English economist said, "If I owe you a pound, I have a problem; but if I owe you a million, the problem is yours."

Real debt is not a partnership. Real debt is using someone else's money to buy something that is either consumed or can't be given back.

In the world of construction, debt is used as a financial tool all the time. A plumber gets a new job, goes to the local hardware store and buys a load of pipe (on credit, as a debt), then he cuts it all up and installs it under the slab of a building. If the owner fails to pay the plumber for his work, the plumber has no money to pay his debt to the hardware store and the store is now in a tough spot. They can't get their money back from a plumber who has no money, and they can't demolish the foundation to retrieve all their cut up pipe. The plumber is indebted to the hardware store and ethically required to pay. If the plumber never pays his debt, it's no different than stealing, and the store should pursue some sort of remedy.

This is the way our credit cards work—the most common form of debt today. I am old enough to recall when credit cards were scarce and we had to carry a wallet full of cash, or produce a checkbook and spend a minute or two writing the name of the store, the amount of the purchase (in both numerical and written form) and then sign our name. We would have to wait until the store "cleared" the check before walking out with our goods. What a pain to wait so long!

Now we swipe our cards across the magic pad and walk away with all kinds of goodies in just a few seconds—food, clothing, appliances, you name it. (I love technology.) Then these nice credit card guys send us a list of the things we purchased over the last month, all totaled at bottom. And when we pay this amount in the required time, we've just used the credit card as an expense organizing service. But when we don't have the money, they are nice enough to allow us to pay only a portion of the month's purchases, but then they add loads of interest and fees. When that happens, we have just entered the real world of debt. We purchased something with their money and we used it up by eating it, or wearing it. If we don't pay it back, it could be considered stealing. But because it's so easy, it becomes habit forming—especially around Christmas time.

PATIENCE

In my opinion, the real problem with debt is not the exchange or goods and services for money you don't have at the time. That's just a risk you and the credit card companies have decided to take. They wouldn't give you the card if they didn't think you could pay.

The problem isn't with risk. The problem with real debt is our hearts. We are not content, we are impatient.

Instead of saving and waiting until we have enough money to buy something, we presume we'll have enough money in the future and risk our monetary security (and possibly our integrity) for immediate gratification. We don't just want it, we want it now. But God is a patient being, and Godliness is patient.

"But the fruit of the spirit is love, joy, peace, patience..." (Galatians 5:22)

"The end of the matter is better than it's beginning, and patience is better than pride." (Ecclesiastes 7:8)

"The Lord is not slow in keeping his promise, as some understand slowness. He is patient with you, not wanting anyone to perish, but everyone to come to repentance." (2 Peter 3:9)

FAITH AND TEMPTING GOD

Going into debt, real debt and not a partnership, is risky because we presume we'll have the money when it's time to pay the bill. We make a bold assumption that our job will be there tomorrow and no new expenses will surprise us—like a car wreck or illness. Some would call this living by faith, but others would call it "tempting God."

So I have a question when it comes to risk and debt. When do we cross the line in having faith that God will provide for our future financial needs, and move into the world of tempting God?

I was once part of a church fundraiser. The church was building a new building and needed pledges from its congregation to finance the project. In order to secure funding the

214

pastor requested what he called "faith pledges"—each person in the congregation was to pray and decide what amount they would pledge for the project, not based on what they believed they could pay, but what God had put on their hearts. "Not to worry," the pastor said. "Just write on the pledge card the amount you think God wants you to put down and then pray and wait for God to provide it."

Is this acting with real faith or is it tempting God?

I had several friends who invested heavily in a Christian night club as an alternative for college students to enjoy on the weekend. They prayed and felt God leading them to invest (and by the way, they had some pressure from other Christian friends as well). After a year of losing money, the place closed and all their investments were lost. They prayed and worked hard for months to make it all work, but it was a bad business plan. The club was not located in a marketable place, and there wasn't a good rotations of music.

There is truly a fine line between acting in faith and tempting God with a bad business plan or a fundraising plan based on the bold presumption that God will provide beyond your means.

Jesus after a long fast was taken to a high hill and pressured by the devil himself.

"Then the devil took him to the holy city and had him stand on the highest point of the temple. 'If you are the Son of God,' he said, 'throw yourself down. For it is written: 'He will command his angels concerning you, and they will lift you up in their hands, so that you will not strike your foot against a stone.' Jesus answered him, 'It is also written: 'Do not put the Lord your God to the test.'" (Matthew 4:5-7)

I have a feeling Jesus could have jumped (thrown himself down) and the angels would have actually come to his rescue, but that crossed the line for him. It would have been a prideful and vulgar display.

Faith is a confidence and conviction in the character and

reality of God. It may be big and bold or it may be in small things, but faith is always accompanied by confidence and grounded in God's character, revealed to us in scripture. Faith never pushes us to take risks based on desires for things and to go into real debt.

When it comes to our money and our livelihood we should be patient and Godly. And we should be good stewards with the resources God has given us. Going into actual debt is a risky venture—bordering on tempting God. So be careful, some things are hard enough to learn by themselves without pressuring God to intervene and learning a doubly hard lesson.

TAKE IT TO THE BANK

Just like our businesses rely on a complex electrical system of power to function (computers, satellites, etc.) our modern financial system relies on a complex system of money and debt to function. If the electrical system shuts down, our world would turn off. And in a very similar way, if our money and debt system stopped functioning, so would the current business world—causing such a financial heart attack that our business bodies may never recover. We would have to be revived though several shocks to the heart, or restart with a whole new body. Certainly we should be as diligent to maintain our monetary systems as a submarine should maintain its air supply, but our faith ultimately is not in our money, but the God who holds the economic world in his hands.

"For this reason I say to you, do not be worried about your life, as to what you will eat or what you will drink; nor for your body, as to what you will put on... But seek first His kingdom and His righteousness, and all these things will be added to you." (Matthew 6:25-33)

There are many of us with little money or resources, but when we compare ourselves to our wealthy neighbors we sometimes long for an equitable adjustment in lifestyle. And the advertisements we see every minute tempt us to make those adjustments using credit cards to spend tomorrows money today. Instead we should compare ourselves to the needy, the sick and starving, and be grateful for the grace shown us.

This type of comparison happened way back in the New Testament times when Paul was taking an offering for the churches in need.

"And now, brothers, we want you to know about the grace that God has given the Macedonian churches. Out of the most severe trial, their overflowing joy and their extreme poverty welled up in rich generosity. For I testify that they gave as much as they were able, and even beyond their ability." (2 Corinthians 8:1-3)

The Macedonians were poor, but they compared themselves to the churches in need and found they were rich enough to give. Even a man with only one meal can cut it in half when he sees his starving neighbor.

Paul tells Timothy, "Instruct those who are rich in this present world not to be conceited or to fix their hope on the uncertainty of riches, but on God, who richly supplies us with all things to enjoy. Instruct them to do good, to be rich in good works, to be generous and ready to share, storing up for themselves the treasure of a good foundation for the future, so that they may take hold of that which is life indeed." (1 Timothy 6:17-19)

16

Employers, Employees and Servanthood

"Recently, I was asked if I was going to fire an employee who made a mistake that cost the company $600,000. No, I replied, I just spent $600,000 training him. Why would I want somebody to hire his experience?" Thomas J. Watson, founder of IBM

"Do not underestimate your abilities. That is your boss's job. Go the extra mile—it makes your boss look like an incompetent slacker." Anonymous (before his first firing)

"It's not so much how busy you are, but why you are busy. The bee is praised, the mosquito is swatted." Anonymous (during his second job)

PARABLE OF THE SHREWD MANAGER

"Jesus told his disciples: 'There was a rich man whose manager was accused of wasting his possessions. So he called him in and asked him, 'What is this I hear about you? Give an account of your management, because you cannot be manager any longer.' The manager said to himself, 'What shall I do now? My master is taking away my job. I'm not strong enough to dig, and I'm ashamed to beg—I know what I'll do so that, when I lose my job here, people will welcome me into their houses.'

"So he called in each one of his master's debtors. He asked the first, 'How much do you owe my master?' 'Eight hundred gallons of olive oil,' he replied. The manager told him, 'Take your bill, sit down quickly, and make it four hundred.' Then he asked the second, 'And how much do you owe?' 'A thousand bushels of wheat,' he replied. He told him, 'Take your bill and make it eight hundred.'"

When the rich man returned, he "commended the dishonest manager because he had acted shrewdly. For the people of this world are more shrewd in dealing with their own kind than are the people of the light." (Luke 16: 1-8)

This parable Jesus told has always bothered me. Here is a guy, an employee (a manager) in the owner's business who is wasteful and bad enough to fire. So when he gets his pink slip and asked to clean out his desk and give an account of this clients, instead of leaving, he slips out the back and makes some deals with the boss' clients (actually steals from him by forgiving some debt), all with the selfish motive of having those guys like him enough to hire him later—to "welcome him into their houses." His boss comes back, and instead of having him arrested, the boss compliments him! This is just not right.

But wait, it appears to get worse. After all this, Jesus tells part of the moral of the story. The people of light (those who love God and desire to please and honor him) could learn a lesson from this guy and the "people of the world."

SLY

First, let's make sure we understand the characters here. In many of his parables, Jesus describes himself as the master. But in this one he is not. The man is described as a rich man with a lazy but sly manager. (And, by the way, this rich man must be very rich. Who but a very rich man could just shrug off half what was owed him?)

Have you ever seen someone do something very sly, and very wrong, but their creativity left you thinking, "Wow!

There's no way I could ever justify doing something like that. But that was ingenious!" It reminds me of the man who stole millions of dollars, flew his small plane into the mountains and parachuted to safety as his plane crashed, leaving everyone to believe he was killed. He is probably still living like a king in a small South American village.

This guy was shrewd, but definitely not innocent. He was creative and crafty, but he was definitely not blameless.

That's how the boss sees his manager, and compliments him for his shrewdness. The manager knew he was getting fired and needed another job. He was not strong enough to do manual labor and he was too ashamed to beg (although he was not too ashamed to steal), so he made some deals. I wonder if the guys he struck the deals with knew he did it without his boss' permission. Would they ever want to do business with him again? The trust thing is rather important … but I digress.

Jesus tells those disciples listening to his parable that he wishes they were as creative with their lives as this guy was—crafty, smart and shrewd, but it is strongly implied that they be innocent also. Jesus is asking for focus and creativity, not immorality.

EMPLOYMENT IN BIBLICAL TIMES

As you would guess, today's world of economics and commerce are very different than biblical times. The idea of a multinational corporation had not even been thought of. Although Alexander the Great had multinational aspirations, they took the form of military conquest, not economic mergers. If you had a job in biblical times, you probably worked in a family business or for the king. There was not much in between.

Slavery was also different back then. In hard times people would sell themselves as slaves (indentured servants or bond servants) to earn food and housing. There were also imprisoned slaves imported from conquered foreign countries—property to buy and sell, much like the slavery we knew before the Civil War. The concept of an employee with medical benefits, payroll taxes, and a 401K retirement plan is a very recent one, but the concept of labor for hire (similar to slavery in biblical times) has been around since there was more work to do than one person could perform. The concept of slavery in the Bible is the closest relationship we have to employment, and with the exception of a whip, the concept of master and slave, employer and employee have changed very little.

If you recall way back at the beginning of this book, we pondered the question why—why are we here, why do we work. If we understand the reason why, we can understand what we ought to do and what we ought not do. We gain a set of guiding principles for the topic at hand.

Well, one question regarding the current chapter is, "Why are there employees and employers?" And what guiding principles spring forward when we answer this why question?

The simple reason why there are employees and employers is that there is work to be done that requires more than one person. If one person could do it all then no other help would be needed—and no one would be needed for employment. But as soon as there is more work than one person can handle, an assistant, a helper, a worker needs to be employed. After, and only after, a person is employed can an employer exist (there is no such thing as an employer without an employee—no slave without a master). The reason for employees and employers is to work to get something done together.

EMPLOYEES

So now that the why has been answered, we come to the

complicated parts - the who, what, when, how, and how much. Who does what part of the job? How do we accomplish the work? Can we work together affectively—or at all? Who gets dirty and who stays clean? Only when you start working together does it get complicated—relationships are always messy. The devil is definitely in the details.

Luckily the first part of the relationship problem is straight forward. The person who needs the help is the one in charge—this guy is the employer and the person hired is the employee. Employees are to work for their employers, and this creates a special relationship between the two—a subordinate relationship.

"Slaves, obey your earthly masters with respect and fear, and with sincerity of heart, just as you would obey Christ. Obey them not only to win their favor when their eye is on you, but like slaves of Christ, doing the will of God from your heart. Serve wholeheartedly, as if you were serving the Lord, not men, because you know that the Lord will reward everyone for whatever good he does, whether he is slave or free." (Ephesians 6:5—8)

It's interesting that Paul in his letter to the Ephesians has a special note for the slaves in that church. The interesting part is that there actually were slaves who were part of the church—there was no distinction because of their race or class, they were part of the church along with the wealthy and well connected. Their value was related to who they were as people made in the image of God, not what they did for work—they were fellow believers but they were still slaves / employees.

In this verse Paul also makes a connection between their work and their calling—he blurs the lines between the worldly work of their everyday life and their spiritual work of the church. "Obey your earthly masters ... with sincerity of heart... like slaves of Christ, doing the will of God from your heart." Obeying your master or employer with sincerity of heart is doing the will of God.

Paul tells Titus, "Teach slaves to be subject to their masters in everything, to try to please them, not to talk back to them, and not to steal from them, but to show that they can be fully trusted, so that in every way they will make the teaching about God our Savior attractive." (Titus 2:9-10)

Pleasing your master or employer and being trusted makes the teaching about God attractive. You're not just working for your boss, you are working on the behalf of God.

Peter also says we slaves not only ought to obey our nice and agreeable masters, we're supposed to obey our difficult masters—for the same reason.

"Slaves, submit yourselves to your masters with all respect, not only to those who are good and considerate, but also to those who are harsh." (I Peter 2:18)

And Paul tells Timothy that slaves who have Godly bosses have a special command.

"Those who have believing masters are not to show less respect for them because they are brothers. Instead, they are to serve them even better, because those who benefit from their service are believers, and dear to them." (1 Timothy 6:2)

All this doesn't sound like slaves or employees have unfulfilling jobs, they actually have a special calling—to serve. And scripture doesn't say they should always stay slaves or employees (thank God we can move up the company ladder as our skills and connections change), but while they are slaves and employees, they are to serve with their whole heart.

EMPLOYERS

As I write this, I can almost hear the question from the employee's side, "What about the masters and employers? What kind of, 'obey just as you would Christ' burden does scripture throw at them?"

First, I hope you don't think obedience is a burden. If you've learned anything from all these chapters I hope you understand that we do everything overflowing from a desire to please and honor God, not from guilt or burden. As we've discussed, John tells us that the essence of the "love of God" is to do what he wants, and the proof is that doing what he wants is not burdensome. You can do what your father asks because you have to or because you want to—you love to. Obeying because you have to is evidence that you may not really love your father.

But when in comes to masters and employers, I don't think they have it as easy as slaves and employees might think. In fact, masters and employers are in reality merely slaves and employees too. Everyone answers to someone with very few exceptions. Your boss answers to his boss and that boss eventually answers to the owner of the company. And the owner of the company answers to the people who buy their products. Even in a large company, the CEO answers to the board of directors and the board of directors answers to the stockholders. The stockholders answer to the federal government and the federal government answers to citizens of the U.S.—supposedly. Everyone answers to someone, so in many ways we are all slaves and employees who ought to "obey just as you would Christ."

However, there are some verses that speak directly to men and women who have the position of masters and employers.

"Slaves, obey your earthly masters ... with sincerity of heart, just as you would obey Christ... Serve wholeheartedly, as if you were serving the LORD... And masters, treat your slaves in the same way. Do not threaten them, since you know that he who is both their Master and yours is in heaven, and there is no favoritism with him." (Ephesians 6:5-9)

We employers are to treat our employees the same way they should treat us—serving them. It appears we are to be mutual servants. We are to serve one another—slave and master, employer and employee. For those who see employment as a way to climb to the top and use their fellow employees as rungs on the ladder, those who take undue credit for the work of subordinates, or those who's desire is to advance at all costs, you have it all backward. In our work and attitude, we should serve each other.

SAME HEART – DIFFERENT ROLES

I recall a television skit, set in a plush executive high-rise office where a boss was having a serious talk with an employee. Right in the middle of the discussion the boss hopped up, opened the filing cabinet behind her and began to file the pile of papers on her large desk—all the while maintaining the conversation with the employee. After filing the papers, the boss went to the closet, brought out a mop and began mopping the floors, then she grabbed the trash and left the room, never stopping the conversation. Finally as the employee was about to leave, the window washing equipment traveled by the window. The boss then opened the window and climbed onto the scaffold and began washing windows. The camera faded with the boss washing windows and the conversation never ending.

When I describe the idea of mutual servanthood, I worry some envision a general in the heat of battle leaving his important command post and running into combat. The sentiment is nice, but who would guide the other troops? The result of a boss doing every job or a general leaving hit post would be chaos.

Mutual servanthood isn't chaotic, it's actually rather poetic. Masters serve their slaves by performing their mastering—and slaves serve their masters by slaving. An employer has certain duties and the employee has other duties and when each does their separate duties well, they are serving one another, and stuff gets done. We have mutual respect but different roles, and when we perform our roles, we serve each other.

God has brought us to our work with different jobs to do—some are more strategically important than others, but we all have a unique set of jobs. And when we do them, we are meeting each others needs and serving one another. Bosses aren't necessarily smarter or wiser, they may just have different educations, experiences or information.

In fact, the best example of mutual servanthood in regard to servants and masters comes from Jesus himself. Just before he was to leave his closest disciples to be arrested and killed, he performs one of the most humble acts of service.

"It was just before the Passover Feast. Jesus knew that the time had come for him to leave this world and go to the Father. Having loved his own who were in the world, he now showed them the full extent of his love... Jesus knew that the Father had put all things under his power, and that he had come from God and was returning to God; so he got up from the meal, took off his outer clothing, and wrapped a towel around his waist. After that, he poured water into a basin and began to wash his disciples' feet, drying them with the towel that was wrapped around him... When he had finished washing their feet, he put on his clothes and returned to his place. 'Do you understand what I have done for you?' he asked them. 'You call me 'Teacher' and 'Lord,' and rightly so, for that is what I am. Now that I, your Lord and Teacher, have washed your feet, you also should wash one another's feet. I have set you an example that you should do as I have done for you. I tell you the truth, no servant is greater than his master, nor is a messenger greater than the one who sent him. Now that you know these things, you will be blessed if you do them.'" (John 13:1-17)

Jesus, the master of masters, didn't think it beneath him at all to perform the work of the lowliest of slave—washing the dirty, sweaty feet of men who wore sandals all day walking along on the dusty, animal trodden streets of Jerusalem. Jesus, the rabbi of rabbis, the one who, according to his own words, God the "father had put all things under his power"— the master who "no servant is greater than" decided to become a servant to teach his disciples to be mutual servants.

I wonder what kind of blessing Jesus was talking about when he said, "Now that you know these things, you will be blessed if you do them." Some pleasant feeling of spiritual contentment? A closer relationship with the one you serve? A promotion from the employer you make look good by your exceptional work? It's hard to tell, but probably all of the above.

I HIRED A CHRISTIAN!

What if one day your CEO (knowing a happy employee is a productive employee) took you out to lunch and asked you, "What could I do to help you be fulfilled in your work?" Would you tell him, "Well, a couple more days of vacation would help." Or, "I see a corporate swimming pool and lounge in our future."

What if your answer was, "You know, the computers we have are becoming outdated and the software I have at home is much more efficient than what I use at work. If we upgraded, my guess is we'd pay for the change in less than a year, everyone would enjoy work better, and we'd all be more productive."

Who would receive a blessing? The first you or the second you? The mutual servant or the vacationing swimmer?

I think employees and employers who love God and live to please and honor him should be the most valuable people in any company. Along with Dr. Del Tackett in " The Truth Project," I would say the employer who after hiring one would turn to his colleagues and exclaim with pride and pleasure, "I just hired a Christian!" And conversely, I would hope an employee who was hired by a Godly employer would smile and tell his friends, "My boss is a Christian!"

"For the people of this world are more shrewd in dealing with their own kind than are the people of the light." (Luke 16: 1-8)

Jesus said this as though he wished his followers were as shrewd as the dishonest manager. By being an employee or employer who knows our roles, and does them with focus and heart, as though working for God, I think we could fulfill Jesus' wish for "the people of light" to be even more shrewd, Godly and productive than the "people of this world." And we could change the entirety of business by doing so.

17

While the Master is Away

"You can't live a perfect day without doing something for someone who will never be able to repay you." John Wooden, UCLA head basketball coach winning 10 straight national championships in 12 seasons

"Worship isn't a means to an end, but the end to all means." RC Sproul, theologian, writer, founder Legonier Ministries

"I long to accomplish great and noble tasks, but it is my chief duty to accomplish humble tasks as though they were great and noble. The world is moved along, not only by the mighty shoves of its heroes, but also by the aggregate of the tiny pushes of each honest worker." Helen Keller, author, lecturer, the first deaf and blind person to earn a bachelors degree, also the subject of the 1962 film The Miracle Worker

MY STORY

Back when I began to discover I was the athletic mutant of my family, I discovered something else. It was around my 14th year when my life began to blossom. Before then everything in it was fairly normal—actually better than what most would call normal. My father loved my mother, my mother loved my father, I was making As in school, I had a lovely girlfriend, and football had made me popular not only in my class but with upperclassmen.

It wasn't the perfect life. There were standard sibling issues and trouble with the world, just like there are today, but

I was oblivious to them. My life was in a good place, except for one thing—I was empty. It's amazing when you get all you think you want, how you realize those things are not fulfilling. It was around this time that my girlfriend invited me to her church.

Since my family had left the church when I was around 8 years old, I happily avoided the place myself, although discussions on spirituality and religion were not banned from home or family gatherings, and we still sought the truth. We just sought them in different venues.

Blaise Pascal, the noted 17th century French mathematician and philosopher, coined the term that described my life at the time. Through the short years of my peaceful and blessed time on earth, there had formed in me an emptiness. Pascal described it as, "A God-shaped vacuum."

And not only was I empty, I had a moral problem (of course I had a moral problem. I was a 14 year old male with raging hormones and a creative imagination similar to every other 14 year old male on the planet). But I also knew that just because it was common to have moral problems, it wasn't right. I had no excuses. There were no deep dark secrets to confess and there was nothing worthy of the National Inquirer. I just knew deep down in my heart that I wasn't the young man I should be and that added to my emptiness.

It was at that church that I learned and embraced the concept of Grace. I learned it by hearing about the life and teachings of unquestionably one of the most influential persons who ever to walked the planet—Jesus of Nazareth. I was guilty and I knew it. I compared my life to what it ought to be and it fell short. I was empty and I knew it. I had everything this 14 year old life desired and all those things fell short of satisfying. Let's just say I found the answers—I found the truth for the first time and I was never the same.

Since that time I have been enamored with the life and teachings of Jesus. I doubt any truthful historian or philosopher could argue the fact that Jesus was the seminal person in world, religious, or political history. It is no accident that the dates we use to mark our years are tied to his birth. Now thousands of years past the event the terms B.C. and A.D. (even B.C.E. and A.C.E, Before and After the Common Era) are related to his life. Muhammad and Muslims refer to Jesus in the Koran, Judaism and Jews do not deny his place in religious history. And it's no wonder. Jesus wasn't shy about what he thought. I recommend you investigate the life and teachings of Jesus, and the whole idea of truth on your own—how to find it and how to prove it. There is no greater quest.

The reason for this book is not to proselytize, evangelize or get into the details of Protestant, Catholic, Orthodoxy or Unorthodoxy, although I definitely have a point of view. This book is a discussion about the meaning behind our work.

WHAT IS COMING

Jesus was in the Temple area when some of his disciples came up and pointed out the beautiful Temple building. You can almost see the wheels turning in Jesus' head when he looked up at the most impressive building in the country and said, with a strange sense of authority, that sometime in the future the entire Temple will be destroyed so severely that not one stone would be left on top of another.

Well, as you might think, this raised a few questions in the disciple's minds.

"Tell us, when will all this happen?" the disciples asked. (Matthew 24:3)

When answering, Jesus gave them much more than they bargained for. He spoke about coming wars, rumors of wars, false teachers and climate distresses. Then, as he wrapped up his talk, he told two parables and a tale of caution.

I believe Jesus knew what was about to happen. Within a few days he would be arrested and killed, and he wanted to give those few men and women remaining with him a glimpse into the future—what to expect and how they should act.

Jesus speaks of the Kingdom of Heaven, but not as a place we go after we die. He uses the phrase as a description of the present world those who love God will live in—day to day. Two parables and a cautionary tale suggest how his followers should live while he was away. And they give insight into how we should live our lives here in the 21st century.

THE BRIDEGROOM AND THE BRIDESMAIDS

The first of the parables is in Matthew 25:1-13.

"The Kingdom of Heaven can be illustrated by the story of ten bridesmaids who took their lamps and went to meet the bridegroom. Five of them were foolish, and five were wise. The five who were foolish took no oil for their lamps, but the other five were wise enough to take along extra oil. When the bridegroom was delayed, they all lay down and slept. At midnight they were roused by the shout, 'Look, the bridegroom is coming! Come out and welcome him!' All the bridesmaids got up and prepared their lamps. Then the five foolish ones asked the others, 'Please give us some of your oil because our lamps are going out.' But the others replied, 'We don't have enough for all of us. Go to a shop and buy some for yourselves.' But while they were gone to buy oil, the bridegroom came, and those who were ready went in with him to the marriage feast, and the door was locked. Later, when the other five bridesmaids returned, they stood outside, calling, 'Sir, open the door for us!' But he called back, 'I don't know you!"

After this story Jesus turns to his disciples and says, "So stay awake and be prepared, because you do not know the day or hour of my return."

Parables are stories told to explain a point—an example or an illustration, a special way of getting to the heart of a matter. Instead of just saying, "Expect me to come back, and here is what I want you to be while I'm away," Jesus tells some stories.

In this parable Jesus refers to himself as the bridegroom, and he refers to 10 young women, bridesmaids, who are waiting for the wedding. None know when the bridegroom will come. But some were prepared and others were not. Those who were prepared for his return made it into the wedding feast, but those who were not, even though they were just as excited to go as the others, were turned away.

The point of the parable? Jesus is alluding to a time when he will actually return. He is alluding to a wedding when his bride (meaning the church—those who love and trust him), and the bridegroom (Jesus himself) will meet and have a great wedding celebration. And he alludes to the sorrowful fact that there will be people awaiting his return who will not be ready—and they will be left out.

THE MASTER AND SERVANTS

The very next parable follows in Matthew 25:14-30 (we've referred to this one before).

"Again, the Kingdom of Heaven can be illustrated by the story of a man going on a trip. He called together his servants and gave them money to invest for him while he was gone. He gave five bags of gold to one, two bags of gold to another, and one bag of gold to the last—dividing it in proportion to their abilities—and then left on his trip.

"The servant who received the five bags of gold began immediately to invest the money and soon doubled it. The servant with two bags of gold also went right to work and doubled the money. But the servant who received the one bag of gold dug a hole in the ground and hid the master's money for safekeeping.

"After a long time their master returned from his trip and called them to give an account of how they had used his money. The servant to whom he had entrusted the five bags of gold said, 'Sir, you gave me five bags of gold to invest, and I have doubled the amount.' The master was full of praise. 'Well done, my good and faithful servant. You have been faithful in handling this small amount, so now I will give you many more responsibilities. Let's celebrate together!' Next came the servant who had received the two bags of gold, with the report, 'Sir, you gave me two bags of gold to invest, and I have doubled the amount.' The master said, 'Well done, my good and faithful servant. You have been faithful in handling this small amount, so now I will give you many more responsibilities. Let's celebrate together!' Then the servant with the one bag of gold came and said, 'Sir, I know you are a hard man, harvesting crops you didn't plant and gathering crops you didn't cultivate. I was afraid I would lose your money, so I hid it in the earth and here it is.' But the master replied, 'You wicked and lazy servant! You think I'm a hard man, do you, harvesting crops I didn't plant and gathering crops I didn't cultivate? Well, you should at least have put my money into the bank so I could have some interest. Take the money from this servant and give it to the one with the ten bags of gold.

"To those who use well what they are given, even more will be given, and they will have an abundance. But from those who are unfaithful, even what little they have will be taken away. Now throw this useless servant into outer darkness, where there will be weeping and gnashing of teeth."

Many of us have heard this story since we were children, exhorting us to use our special talents in a way that God would be pleased. It's called the Parable of the Talents, but the simple message we've heard as children misses some important points—points very pertinent to us in the business world.

The writers used the term "bag of gold" instead of talent. The English word "talent" is different than the one used today. In biblical times, a talent was an amount of money, around 100 denarii, which was about a year's wages for a normal laborer. It wasn't until the 1400s that the word talent changed to mean your abilities.

Jesus describes himself as the master (the owner of the estate) going on a trip and he has three servants he trusts with his money—enough to invest for him while he's gone.

How did he hand out the talents (bags of gold)? He gave them to each servant according to their abilities—according to their talents. He knew who these guys were, knew what they were capable of, and invested in them accordingly. The story is more about money, investing and accountability than the distribution of abilities or talents.

What did the first two servants do with the money? They immediately began investing according to their abilities. They may have been carpenters or cobblers—who knows. They may have been bankers or merchants. All we know is they were talented servants who were ready and eager to invest. And what do you do when you invest money? You put it at risk. You buy wood and tools to build cabinets, or you buy leather and string and make shoes—with the risk that no one will want to buy what you make.

The story is a contrast between the two good servants and a bad one. The good servants immediately put their master's money to work. They were comfortable with the trust of their master and their own abilities. But the bad servant for some reason just buried the money—we assume to keep it safe.

At first glance, the bad servant doesn't look all that bad. He just looks a bit cautious—at least he didn't take the master's money and spend it on a magic beans or lavish parties. But it's only after the Master returns that we see the heart of this guy and what he did wrong.

This servant isn't cautious, he actually doesn't like the master. In fact, he insults him—calls him a thief. "Sir, I know you are a hard man, harvesting crops you didn't plant and gathering crops you didn't cultivate ..." No wonder the master took his money away.

The point of this parable? For one, just like the bride-groom in the first parable, the boss who goes away will actually return. He will come back, even after a long time.

Another point is that we geniuses who are active in the business world may actually be blessed with money to invest in our businesses, our families, our churches, and we should do just that—invest. Put it wisely at risk. Use our talents, all the while keeping in mind that the master expects a return on that investment.

And as we have discussed previously in other chapters, the money we earn is not our own. We have just been given use of it for a while—it's a test. It belongs to the boss and we earn big profits knowing full well that we will return it to its rightful owner. What does the master want with our money or profit? You'll see next with the sheep and goats.

And finally, if you are ungrateful, actually dislike and de-sire not to be with the master, don't expect to be welcomed when he returns. You should expect to go where you would rather be, away from where the master lives.

THE SHEEP AND GOATS

Finally Matthew 25: 31-46.

"But when the Son of Man comes in his glory, and all the angels with him, then he will sit upon his glorious throne. All the nations will be gathered in his presence, and he will separate them as a shepherd separates the sheep from the goats. He will place the sheep at his right hand and the goats at his left.

"Then the King will say to those on the right, 'Come, you who are blessed by my Father, inherit the Kingdom prepared for you from the foundation of the world. For I was hungry, and you fed me. I was thirsty, and you gave me a drink. I was a stranger, and you invited me into your home. I was naked, and you gave me clothing. I was sick, and you cared for me. I was in prison, and you visited me.' Then these righteous ones will reply, 'Lord, when did we ever see you hungry and feed you? Or thirsty and give you something to drink? Or a stranger and show you hospitality? Or naked and give you clothing? When did we ever see you sick or in prison, and visit you?' And the King will tell them, 'I assure you, when you did it to one of the least of these my brothers and sisters, you were doing it to me!'

"Then the King will turn to those on the left and say, 'Away with you, you cursed ones, into the eternal fire prepared for the Devil and his demons! For I was hungry, and you didn't feed me. I was thirsty, and you didn't give me anything to drink. I was a stranger, and you didn't invite me into your home. I was naked, and you gave me no clothing. I was sick and in prison, and you didn't visit me.' Then they will reply, 'Lord, when did we ever see you hungry or thirsty or a stranger or naked or sick or in prison, and not help you?' And he will answer, 'I assure you, when you refused to help the least of these my brothers and sisters, you were refusing to help me.' And they will go away into eternal punishment, but the righteous will go into eternal life."

These are tough words—the truth can hurt sometimes.

Jesus refers to himself as the Son of Man many times in scripture, so he is talking about himself in this story, coming with angels. He refers to himself as the King sitting on the thrown with the authority and wisdom to separate people and nations like sheep and goats.

Then he says the strangest thing—at least to my mind. He speaks of the people who fed and clothed those in need. He tells of those who were hospitable to strangers and those who cared for the sick. And he tells of those who visited people in prison.

It's not that doing these things is so strange to me—they are the things people who love God and live to please and honor him do automatically. What's strange, and I love it, is that the sheep were surprised to hear it ... "Who me? I was just doing what came naturally - what I desired to do."

Another strange thing is that Jesus said while they were doing these things for others, they were doing them for him at the same time.

The nature of the spiritual and physical worlds are a fascinating mystery. Even Paul describes seeing these things as through a foggy glass. There is some strange physical/spiritual connections I don't fully understand I think we in the western world make the line between spiritual and physical too rigid—a left over from our Greek philosophical heritage. Those who wrote scripture had very little of such a heritage. The Jews grew up with an eastern heritage. They merged the spiritual and physical more than we westerners do, and at times it's a hindrance to our understanding of scripture.

Jesus is saying there is a direct connection between our actions and spiritual world. When we act with compassion to people in true need, we are doing these things for and to him. After I die, I think the first question I will have for God will be about how spirituality and physicality relate—or maybe it will be obvious after I'm there.

The upside is great, the sheep will be with the King. But the downside is as tragic as anything. There are those who see the needs of people and have the ability and wherewithal to help, but they won't. And in the same strange way, they deny Christ the same things others provide.

I don't think the point of the story is a call to rush out and feed all the hungry, house all the homeless, and so on. Problems with hunger, homelessness, and imprisonment require much more than quick, temporary fixes. Missionaries and social workers alike will tell you it is best to teach and resource a person to grow their own food than just to satisfy their hunger. But a good case can be made that our activities in the world of business fulfill most of these needs. In many countries, there are private and public institutions to meet the basic necessities of our neighbors who are needy. But the rest of the world is a different, more complex and a tragic story filled with corruption, both private and governmental, denying the needs their own people.

THE CONCLUSION TO THE MATTER

What are we to do while the bridegroom, the master, the Son of Man, Jesus, is away? What does Jesus say he wants us to do while we remain here?

If you love God, you will eagerly await his return. But if you don't love God, you will deny or dread it. He is coming soon and we should be prepared for it like the bridesmaids.

And like the Master's servants, we should gladly take the money, possessions, and the wealth he has entrusted us with, invest them according to our talents and make a profit, knowing full well that we are creating profit for the benefit of the master and not ourselves.

And finally we take this profit and look for the ways to use it with compassion. Our hearts focused on others, those in true need and those we love—our families, pastors, ministers, missionaries, nonprofits and for profits alike—whoever serves those truly in need. While the master is away, we should be involved in the world of commerce, making use and trading all the gifts or resources we have been blessed with. We should be active in the world, getting involved with our neighbors through service, trade or production.

Look back over your life. You've been involved in the world of trade and commerce since you first began to speak. You've traded up—your time for education which you trade in the marketplace of ideas and commerce. And if you were successful in your trading, you may have doubled, tripled or multiplied your investments times ten, like the good servants did.

But while the master is gone, our mission is not to focus entirely on ourselves and business. We are to be aware of the world and the needs around us. A compassionate heart isn't focused on the profit of work, it's been trained to see the needs of the individuals in the workplace or those outside the marketplace. And Jesus exhorts us not to just see the needs but to meet them. And in so doing, we are mysteriously and literally serving Christ.

Paul adds to this idea in his letter to the Corinthians, "Now he who supplies seed to the sower and bread for food will also supply and increase your store of seed and will enlarge the harvest of your righteousness. You will be made rich in every way so that you can be generous on every occasion, and through us your generosity will result in thanksgiving to God. This service that you perform is not only supplying the needs of God's people but is also overflowing in many expressions of thanks to God. Because of the service by which you have proved yourselves, men will praise God for the obedience that accompanies your confession of the gospel of Christ, and for your generosity in sharing with them and with everyone else. And in their prayers for you their hearts will go out to you, because of the surpassing grace God has given you." (2 Corinthians 9: 10-14)

What does God give to those who work for him? He doesn't miraculously create more food or a bigger harvest. He gives them more seed—more seed to plant, more money to invest, more work to do for him.

We should certainly save for rainy days, the education of our children, or for food and housing in our retirement. It isn't a sin to be blessed with a windfall profit in a public offering of stock, or other forms of wealth. But when we see a legitimate need in our neighbor, we should consider diverting our wealth in order to wisely meet that need, whether through temporary emergency relief or permanent dignified opportunities for employment, education, or investment—

all tools to leverage our wealth for Godly opportunities.

Should we go as far as to give away the seed we need to plant future crops? No, it would be foolish. We would all eventually starve.

I have a confession to make. I didn't just write this book as a lesson for students and young business men and women. I wrote it for myself. My world can be so complicated and my random thoughts so scattered regarding my work in relation to God's work, that I needed to study and write this book, for me to understand these concepts.

There is an enormous amount of wealth in this world—both actual and potential, monetary and creative. But the problems are too large: poverty and genocide in Africa, child abduction and slavery in the Far East, nuclear negotiations, and the growing globalization of commerce. What in the world can "I" do—what can "we" do?

We can be wise and strategic!

We all have resources, whether time, money, talent, or all three. And when I realize that one individual in Austin, Texas can affect a random soul in the fields of China through modern commerce, it is possible to affect every individual in the entire world with simple yet extraordinary works of Godliness.

The world is becoming smaller, and the problems of the world are getting closer with the advancement of communications and media. We can't help but think globally.

"Think Globally, Act Locally," was a phrase coined in the 1960s. How true it is for today. But I would like to change the wording a bit. How about "Think Eternally, Act Temporally," or "Think Shrewdly, Act Innocently?" Not as catchy, but for me it holds a better perspective.

The problem of hunger needs more than a plane full of food. The problem of poverty is bigger than money. Jesus said with compassion but realism, "the poor you will always have with you." Evil and injustice throughout the world, geo-political economics and world banks negotiating human rights are bigger than me.

The problems of the world are not economic. Economic systems come and go with the ages—Feudalism, Capitalism, Communism, Socialism, etc. The haves and have-nots continue to struggle, and attempts at mass distribution and redistribution of wealth eventually ends in a bureaucratic labyrinth.

The problems of the world are moral—not economic. Food can't get to the starving because an immoral dictator wants to retain control over his country. Men traveling the world on business look for nightly gratification and create an underworld of corrupt commerce. To make a little more money, a construction worker puts only three bolts onto the beam when he was hired to put on eight to hold properly.

All politics is local and all morality is individual. The problems are not a collective of immoralities, they are all propagated by individuals making individual choices. And no group can or should excuse those choices.

But there is a disconnect even greater than the one between our work and the modern church. We have a disconnect between ourselves and the author of morality, a disconnect of our own choosing. We lean toward our own selfish thoughts and desires. And Jesus says this is why he came to us, to deliver us from ourselves. "For God did not send me into this world to condemn the world, but to save it." "For Christ died for sins once for all, the righteous for the unrighteous, to bring you to God." Jesus had some amazing and disturbing things to say about himself and us. I recommend you read them all.

Not all of us can fly to Bangladesh to feed the poor. Not all of us can influence a monarchy. Not all of us can build a school. But we all can love God, love our neighbors, live to please and honor him, and perform our simple work to influence our world for Godliness.

What person doesn't yearn to know what God wants for

their life? Who, after learning their call to live a life of Godliness and extraordinary good works, shies away from it because they lack the faith or will to follow it? Too many, I'm afraid.

Even after having been given the vision and means to take hold of the work God has prepared for them, many risk their lives for a shot at mere happiness. But how joyful, fulfilled, and meaningful is a life lived in the service of the God who "exercises kindness, justice and righteousness on the earth." A God who delights in these things.

What we need is a change of heart. And not a heart for a "something"—like a revised business strategy or a new economic system, no matter how kind, just or right it is. What we need is a heart for a "someone"—a heart for the heavenly father who exists, has spoken to us through his words in scripture, and who gives us the secret to discovering all he wants of us if we only seek him.

"You will seek me and find me when you seek me with all of your heart" (Jeremiah 29:13)

OTHER RECOMMENDED READING:

Doug Sherman and William Hendricks, Your Work Matters to God (Colorado Springs, CO, NavPress, 1987)

Wayne Grudem, Business for the Glory of God: The Bible's Teachings on the Moral Goodness of Business (Wheaton, IL: Crossway Books: 2003)

Richard Higginson, Questions of Business Life: Exploring Workplace Issues from the Christian Perspective (Waynesboro, GA, Spring Harvest Publishing Division and Authentic Media, 2002)

Alexander Hill, Just Business: Christian Ethics for the Marketplace (Downers Grove, IL, InterVarsity Press, 1997)

Os Guinness, The Call: Finding and Fulfilling the Central Purpose of Your Life (Nashville, TN, W Publishing Group, a division of Thomas Nelson Inc., 1998, 2003)

Randy Alcorn, Money, Possessions and Eternity (Carol Stream, IL, Tyndale House Publishers, Inc. 1989, 2003)

Dennis W. Bakke, Joy at Work: A Revolutionary Approach to Fun on the Job (Seattle, WA, PVG, 2005)

R.C. Sproul, Jr., Biblical Economics: A Commonsense Guide to Our Daily Bread (Bristol, TN, Draught House Press, 1985, 1994, 2002)

Francis A. Schaeffer, He is There and He is not Silent (Carol Stream, IL, Tyndale House Publishers Inc., 1972, 2001)

STUDY AND DISCUSSION QUESTIONS FOR THIS BOOK ARE AVAILABLE AT MARSHILLPUBLISHING.COM